# Notes On Ireland

## And Other Writings

By Nancy Hennessy

Compiled and Edited by Jim Berwick

Copyright © 2010 by Nancy Hennessy

*Notes on Ireland and Other Writings*
by Nancy Hennessy

Printed in the United States of America

ISBN 9781612153582

All rights reserved solely by the author. The author guarantees all contents are original and do not infringe upon the legal rights of any other person or work. No part of this book may be reproduced in any form without the permission of the author. The views expressed in this book are not necessarily those of the publisher.

www.xulonpress.com

# TABLE OF CONTENTS

I.  Introduction ............................... vii

II.  Notes on Ireland (and other
places, people and events)............ 13

III.  Favorite Poems ........................... 75

IV.  Nancy Hennessy's Poems.............. 99

V.  Nancy Hennessy's Short
Stories....................................... 113

VI.  The Innkeeper's Child................ 222

VII.  Editor's Final Note..................... 258

# INTRODUCTION

While growing up, I had many hours of conversations with my aunt Nancy about writing. We exchanged many ideas about titles of books, characters, how to write, etc. I hope to write several mysteries in the future, or at least like Agatha Christie did several times, write several short mysteries and put them into a book. I have plots and storylines and titles for mysteries, and many of them came from the discussions and conversations I had with Aunt Nancy.

While we were talking one day, she just happened to mention that she had done some writing. This was the first I had heard of it. She said that she had some notes on Ireland and other writings, and that she hoped to publish them or make her writings into a book someday.

Notes on Ireland and other writings..... now that she has passed on, I have many of her writings and am putting them together in a book, and the line she said to me will be the title.

After this introduction, I have enclosed some of her notes on Ireland and her notes on other places, people and events. Much of her notes and stories are in her own handwriting, and sometimes it is difficult to read and not very clear. Every effort has been made to include the writing as she wrote it. Also, many of her notes on Ireland have basically been taken from other sources, and much of that has not been included. For example, she had 3 entire notebooks full of notes about the ancient laws of Ireland, and they were taken from the Senchus Mor and other sources. I did not think it was necessary to include those, and only some notes taken from other sources have been used. Again, with it being in her handwriting, every attempt was made to copy what she wrote correctly, and what she took from other sources correctly. This is an ABRIDGED VERSION, with most of her notes not clear enough to use. Her notes from other sources are also NOT VERBATIM.

*Notes on Ireland and Other Writings*

After those notes, I have included some of her favorite poems written by others, and the section after that are her poems.

Following the poems are her short stories. The final two short stories, titled "Tillicum" and "The Moon and Ellen Adele," were previously published in "Spoken In Due Season," from the Writing Class at the Senior Activity Center in Bellingham, WA. It was edited by Dorothy Koert and published in 1979. Nothing has been found regarding publication anywhere else.

On July 21, 1980, the Whatcom County Council on Aging, the sponsors of the Senior Activity Center, wrote my aunt a letter giving her release of the stories and permission to publish in other media. I also acknowledge this copyright, am mentioning that the two stories were previously published, and will mention so again in front of the stories printed here. I am also including a copy of the letter after this introduction.

After the short stories is a longer story, titled "The Innkeeper's Child." In many places, the writing was not clear and not in order. But by using her notes and piecing it together, I am confident that the stories are as she would have wanted them. For this longer story my aunt had several ver-

*Notes on Ireland and Other Writings*

sions that went off in several directions. Hopefully I have made a coherent story out of it.

I conclude the book with a sample of my aunt's handwriting, and then with a final note. I hope you enjoy reading my aunt's work....she lived from March 21, 1905 to December 21, 1986. Her hope of a book didn't happen while she was alive, but hopefully now her writings will live on.

Jim Berwick, nephew

*Notes on Ireland and Other Writings*

## Whatcom County Council on Aging, Inc.

Sponsors of the Senior Activity Center

315 HALLECK STREET
BELLINGHAM, WASHINGTON 98225

TELEPHONE 733-4030

July 21, 1980

Nancy Hennessy
2527 Undine St.
Bellingham, WA 98225

Dear Miss Hennessy:

You have requested the release of your writings which were published in the book <u>Spoken In Due Season</u> which the Whatcom County Council on Aging has obtained the copyrights.

I understand you wish the approval to publish your stories. I have inquired of our legal services and find that release can be given so that your work can be published in other media.

When printing your stories, acknowledgement must be made of the copyright and that approval has been given by the Whatcom County Council on Aging.

This letter should be sufficient in giving that approval.

Cordially,

Catherine May

CM·mf

# NOTES ON IRELAND

(and other places, people and events)

## "Life in Ancient Ireland – The Education of Children"

## by Nancy Hennessy

Fosterage of children was a feature of life among the Irish from the most ancient times. It continued in a modified form down to the seventeenth century at least. It was the closest of bonds between families, and was considered almost a sacred relationship. Fosterage of children was carefully regulated by law, and the duties and rights were minutely detailed.

A child might be sent to live with foster parents at one year of age, where boys were kept until they were seventeen years old, and girls fourteen, when they returned to their own parents, being now of marriage-able age. Fosterage was practiced by people of all classes, but most often by people of high rank. A father sent his child to be raised and educated in the home and with the family of another person or sent him to be fostered by a distinguished scholar, saint or other admirable person.

There were two kinds of fosterage: for friendship and for money. In the first, no payment was made. In the other, the fosterage fee was regulated by the rank of the parties. It was sometimes paid in land, but was usually in cattle. Animals and land were the usual means of payment, though sometimes grain was used.

For the son of the lowest grade of chief, the payment was three cows. For the son of a king, the fee was from eighteen to thirty cows. As girls were considered to be more trouble to rear, requiring greater care, and less able to help the foster parents in later life should they fall into adversity, the fee was accordingly higher. The child at fosterage was treated in every way as a member of the family. There were explicit regulations regarding clothes, food and amusement, all of which varied according to rank. The children of kings, chiefs, poets and so forth were eagerly sought after for fosterage, and so it happened that these children sometimes had two, three or more foster parents. One great chief had nine foster fathers in his childhood. Girls were also sent to foster parents, though not as often as boys.

Fosterage was the closest tie possible between families. Frequently children became more devoted to their foster families than to their own relatives. In the case of children fostered by poets, bards and so forth, all fees earned by the child while at

*Notes on Ireland and Other Writings*

fosterage were to be paid to the tutor, as well as the first fee he earned after leaving him. If the foster parents became impoverished in later life, the foster son was obligated to help and support them. At the end of his fosterage, the foster son received a parting gift from his foster father. The fosterage system, the historians tell us, is probably the forerunner of the English boarding schools.

Bellingham, Washington
September 1977

## "Some Farm Animals in Ireland"

## by Nancy Hennessy

From earliest times, before history began to be recorded, cows were the greatest source of wealth in Ireland. White cows with red ears were considered to be extremely valuable. Next in value to the cow was the pig. Almost everyone kept pigs. Pork was highly valued as a food, and there was always plenty of it.

Feeding pigs was easy and cheap. There were oak forests everywhere in ancient times, and the pigs were turned loose in the woods where they feasted on the meat and any other goodies they might find. They really lived like kings, those ancient Irish pigs. In summer, they were out in the open day and night, but in winter they were kept in pig-sties to protect them from the cold. In autumn was when the mast was on the ground and at the end of autumn, fattening and also the slaughtering took place, so there were not as many pigs left to be kept in the sties.

Sometimes these oak forests were private property, but usually they were part of the "Commons" and every member of the tribe was free to graze his stock there.

*Notes on Ireland and Other Writings*

When woodland was not available, the pigs were fed on corn and sour milk, which was also plentiful. They also were fed on malt-grains.

The old Irish pig was long-snouted, lean, muscular and active, and they scoured the country like hounds.

My grandfather, who came from Ireland shortly before the Civil War, said that the Irish pig, because he was free, was very clean....and that many of the very poor people who could only afford one pig treated him exactly as we do a dog. They are very, very intelligent and respond to human kindness.


Bellingham, Washington
July 1978

## "The Brehons of Ancient Ireland"

## by Nancy Hennessy

In ancient Ireland, a judge was called a Brehon. It is not known how the Brehons happened to have the exclusive right to interpret laws and arbitrate quarrels. They were in existence before the recording of history.

To become a brehon a man had to go through a course of study and training, the same course which qualified for any branch of the legal profession. Once a man completed this course, he might become a judge, a lawyer, or a law-agent. A brehon should also be a historian.

In the most ancient times the brehon was considered to be an inspired person, watched over by a divine power, who would punish him if he gave an unjust decision. In the first century A. D., the great judge Morann wore a metal collar around his neck which tightened when he gave a wrong judgment, and loosened again when he gave the right one. At least that is what the legend tells us.

In the beginning every poet was also a brehon. This lasted until the time of King Conor MacNessa in the first century. Then two poets were arguing a point of law in public, with Conor and his chieftains looking on. Their language was so technical and involved that no one could understand what they meant. Conor became so incensed that he took away from all poets the privilege of also being brehons. The legal profession, no longer confined to poets only, was now open to anyone who could qualify.

Several famous brehons were women. One of these was Brigh. Her decisions established precedents for many centuries.

The brehons continued to flourish until the early part of the 17th century, when the system was abolished by the English invaders, who set up their own special system of legal justice in Ireland.


Bellingham, Washington
July 1978

## "Ancient Ireland's Criminal Law Book"

## by Nancy Hennessy

The Book of Aicill was the book among the ancient Irish dealing with the criminal law. It was composed in the third century by Cormac MacArt, High King of Ireland in that time, and by Cennfaladh, a poet. It came about as follows:

Aicill is the ancient name of the Hill of Skreen, near Tara in County Meath. One of Cormac's sons, named Cellach, abducted the daughter of Sacar, son of Art Corb. Sacar's kinsman, Angus of the Poisoned Spear, was a champion who was at that time avenging a family quarrel in Leyney, County Sligo. He forced his way into a woman's house and drank the milk. She taunted him, "It would be better to avenge your kinswoman up Cellach, than to take my food by force." Angus did no further injury to the woman, but took himself off to Tara, arriving at sunset. After dark no weapons could be brought inside the great Hall of Tara, so Angus took down from its place on the wall the beautifully orna-mented spear of Cormac, father of Cellach. He struck Cellach with the spear and killed

*Notes on Ireland and Other Writings*

him. But the edge of the spear grazed one of Cormac's eyes and destroyed his sight.

It was unlawful in ancient Ireland that anyone with a blemish of any kind should be High King of Erin. And so Cormac was dethroned and his son Carbery of the Lippey was made High King in his place. Cormac was sent to Aicill for treatment of his injury. Carbery admired his father very much, and when he had difficult cases to judge he would go to Aicill and lay the problem before his father. Thus, Cormac formulated *his* part of the Book of Criminal Law. He always prefaced his commentaries thus – "My son, that thou mayest know...." And sometimes preceded by the word "exemption." Thus it is possible to tell what part is his and what part is Cennfaladh's.

Cennfaladh was a young Irish chief who lived almost 400 years later in the reign of Domhnall, who reigned in 612 A. D., when Domhnall fought against his rebellious foster son Congal Claen in the Battle of Magh Rath (Moira). In this battle, Cennfaladh's skull was fractured by an enemy's sword. He was sent to a famous medical college at Tomregan, in County Cavan for treatment. They performed the operation called trefinning on his brain,

*Notes on Ireland and Other Writings*

and he recovered. He was there for a year. He was compelled to give up his military career, and so turned his attention to the law. He was a very brilliant jurist, and the Book of Aicill reflects his many wise decisions.

The entire book consists of precedents – the legal pronouncements of Cennfaladh and Cormac. Cormac eventually recovered his sight and was restored to his position as Monarch of Ireland. He choked to death on a salmon bone, which was an unusual way for an Irish king to die. Most of them died in battle or by assassination.


Bellingham, Washington
June 1978

*Notes on Ireland and Other Writings*

(Editor's note: these notes are in my aunt's handwriting, and sometimes tough to read. I am trusting that the notes are from the source(s) mentioned and every attempt was made to read the handwriting clearly and write as she had it.)

## Notes taken from "All About Ireland" by Creed

"Humanity" Martin - The road from Roundstone is called "the brandy and soda road" because of its air. It goes past Ballynahinch, the old estate of the Martins, who were the great family hereabouts, and pretended to change their religion to suit Cromwell, and so kept their castle and their land and acquired the lands of the O'Flaherties as well. They were on the whole popular and good squires in this hard country. The best known of them was "Humanity" Martin, whose early exploits and prodigality ruined his family, but his later efforts in the British Parliament to prevent the cruel treatment of animals earned him his nickname.

*        *        *        *

Hennessy family - Seven miles north of Mallow (County Cork, Blackwater valley) is Killavullen, on a river crag perches the original home of Hennessy, the first distiller of brandy. The Hennessys emigrated to France with the Dillon Regiment in Patrick Sarsfield's day.

\* \* \* \*

A peasant remarked to Gibbings, who wrote "Lovely is the Lee," that great monuments crumble away but "a pile of stones lasts forever......"

\* \* \* \*

Battle of Moytura fought in 1330 B. C.

Dathi, the last Pagan King of Ireland, is buried under an enclosed tumulus crowned by a red sandstone pillar at the Burial Place of the Kings.

\* \* \* \*

The ancient Irish ascribed the Giant's Causeway to Finn MacCool, who could do anything. Actually a subterranean convulsion along the entire Antrim coast

*Notes on Ireland and Other Writings*

created a quality of molten basalt which cooled under conditions which account for both the symmetry and the columnar structure. The red and ochre formation is composed of prismatic octagonal and hexagonal stones so exactly chiseled that it is very difficult to believe they are a natural formation.

The Glens of Antrim, 9 in number, are a series of romantic valleys running inland from the coast of the North Channel, cutting across the hills that rise between Larne and Ballycastle. They are characterized by wild ravines, woods and waterfalls.

\*   \*   \*   \*

There was the Cornish king, Theodoric, who massacred St. Fingar and his party in Cornwall......

And Cormac MacArt brought the water mill into Ireland to ease the labor of his enslaved concubine, a Pictish princess...

- End of copy from "All About Ireland" by Creed, according to her notes (Abridged Version)

\*   \*   \*   \*

*Notes on Ireland and Other Writings*

(Editor's note: these notes and the next notes, about Monmouthshire, are about Wales and other places. These are in my aunt's handwriting and once again I am trusting that the notes came from the source and every attempt was made to read the writing clearly and write as she wrote it....with some of the old names it is rather difficult.)

## Notes taken from "The Verge of Wales" by Palmer

Apparently King Offa abandoned the Monmouthshire plain to the Welsh, connecting with the Severn along the Gloucestershire side of the river Wye. Today the titanic scarp and counterscarp are seen, to the east of Chepstowe, right on the cliff's edge above the Severn.

The old British (or Welsh) name of Chepstowe was Castell Gwent; the Saxons gave it a name which meant the place of markets or merchandise.

\*    \*    \*    \*

Maiden Castle - on a crossing of the Broxton Hills, has a wide and fine view from the fortress....Maiden Castle on Bickerton

*Notes on Ireland and Other Writings*

Hill, the southern end of the Peckforton Range, had a ditch and rampart guarding it on 2 sides, the steep escarpment and slope on the other.

\* \* \* \*

St. David's Chapel - From the Hereford-Abergavenny road, turn into the Honddu valley and find the ruins of Llanthony. This is an in-and-out journey of about 6 miles either way, on a narrow and twisted countryside which is full of hills and waterworn patches, banks and ditches. There is a sort of village green, and from this a steep short pitch leads up to the church and the ruins of the priory. The full name of the foundation is "the church of David by the river Honddu." In the early Norman conquest an adherent of Hugh de Lacy rode into the wild vale, found the remains of an old chapel of St. David, and rebuilt the chapel.

\* \* \* \*

Caerleon - From Caerwent to Caerleon there were 17 miles of the Via Julia Maritima, an important road which had come from London and Bath by way of

Gloucester or some ancient ferry across Severn. Caerleon was handsomely built of masonry, with courses of bricks, by the Romans. Immense palaces ornamented, a tower of prodigious size, remarkable hot baths, temples and theaters, all enclosed within fine walls, and stoves construed with wonderful art to transmit the heat through narrow tubes passing up the side walls.

In 400 A. D. Caerleon was a great military center, with its 9 miles of circumference, in which were contained the villas of the nobles and the great camp of the famous Second Augustan Legion.

From Caerleon, the road follows the river up to Usk, where formerly was the camp and fortress known as Burrium.

\*   \*   \*   \*

Skirrid Fawr - Encircled on 3 sides by lofty mountains, Abergavenny lies on a plain where the river Gavenny joins the Usk. A crack divides Skirrid Fawr Mountain into 2 unequal parts. From the west it is an enormous chasm separating 2 heights and at its foot, nearly 300 feet wide, are masses of rock broken in some great cataclysm. The story runs that the mountain was cut asunder at the time of the Crucifixion. Sugar Loaf Mountain is nearby.

\* \* \* \*

Abergavenny - Abergavenny is built on or about the site of a Roman station. North of the town Watling Street crossed and at Abbey Dore a small portion of the original Stane Street has been uncovered. The road crossed the Wye west of Hereford, where Magna had been a small Roman town surrounded by a stone wall and was a place of some comfort. On the other hand, Bravonium on the Teme was a stark military post.

\* \* \* \*

Fortified bridges - In some places there were fortified bridges in front of the castletown. Of these, Monnow Bridge, across the river at Monmouth, is the only specimen left in the British Isles of a fortified gateway actually standing on a bridge.

\* \* \* \*

Symonds Yat - (or hill) is 740 feet above the sea and is a limestone outcrop. On a clear day from its height several counties – Gloucester, Monmouth, Hereford and Worcester can be seen, as well as a bit of Wiltshire Downs and some heights of Wales. The Roman general Ostorius is supposed to have stationed his army here for the coal and iron ore in the Forest of Dean.

- End of copy from "the Verge of Wales" by Palmer, according to her notes (Abridged Version)

\* \* \* \*

Re: St. David -

In 519 Cerdic and Cynric became West Saxon Kings after the Battle of Charford won them Hampshire and the Isle of Wight.

Fall of Sarum in 550.

In 563 St. Columba founded the monastery of Iona.

In 577 the Battle of Dyrham was won by the W. Saxons and cut off the Welsh of Cornwall from the Welsh of Wales.

*Notes on Ireland and Other Writings*

\* \* \* \*

## Notes taken from "Monmouthshire" by Arthur Mee

Llanthewy-Vach lies in the hills about 4 miles to the north of Caerleon, with the tiny Soar Brook forming its eastern boundary. One looked over hill and valley and high woods to the church tower on the hill above Caerleon. Through a cleft one might see a bright yellow glint of the Severn sea and the cliffs of Somerset beyond.

Llanvaches is a hilly place lying between Wentwood Forest and the Roman road from Caerwent to Caerleon. There is an ancient camp nearby that was here when Roman legions marched this way. The long ridge of Gray Hill is here. Wild daffodils bloom here in the spring.

Llangstone - the long stone which gives the village its name lies in a field nearly hidden by nettles, on the Newport-Chepstow road. Along the brow of a hillacross the valleynorth of Llangstone runs an old Roman road, the Via Julia; it goes on to Christchurch and then dips down to Caerleon.

\* \* \* \*

St. Brides Netherwent lies in a valley between Wentwood Forest and Caldicot Level. On a tree-clad hill near the village is an ancient camp and not far away is a barrow from the Early Bronze Age (1800 to 1400 B. C.). There is a rushing brook.

St. Brides Wentloog lies beside the Bristol Channel. The fields are bounded by green streams with banks of golden iris, and the roads are lined with little willows. Here too is a stretch of golden sand.

Here is an area of nearly 25,000 acres stretching 20 miles along the coast and 3 miles inland, much of it below high water mark and haunted by the heron. The soil is mainly bluish clay deposited by the tide which formerly reached the old cliff line, traceable behind the levels. Mixed with the clay is sand and gravel brought down by the Usk. The Romans seem to have been the first people to drain these soils for the use of man, and to them is attributed the sturdy wall shutting out the Severn. The main ditches were also cut by the Romans and it is these ditches called reens which form such a feature of the levels. They are up to 6 feet deep and the villagers jump across with long poles.

\* \_\* \* \*

Mathern early became an important place owing to its position on the Severn at a spot where ferries could cross.

Gray Hill is a glorious height of some 900 feet and commanding magnificent views over the Bristol Channel. On the summit are 2 stones, each as high as a man, all that remains of a circle 10 yards across.

The Sugar Loaf (2000 feet) is a landmark for shipping in the Bristol Channel. It is about 15 miles north of Caerleon.

Newport is a place of great antiquity at the mouth of the Usk, the one navigable river in Monmouthshire. There were Britons dwelling here when the Roman legions went sailing by to Caerleon, and Saxon and Danish invaders also came this way. Certainly by the 8th Century a township had grown up here on Stow Hill. In the 5th Century the converted chief of the district, Gwynllyw, built a church here. It was named Newport after the decline of Caerleon. Gwynllyw was a new convert to Christianity, and he later became St. Woolos.

Penterry lies hidden behind the hills which fringe the Wye Valley and the road to it has fine views across the Severn beyond the white cliffs of the Wye. Hidden

*Notes on Ireland and Other Writings*

by the trees on Gaer Hill is an old earthwork. Penterry is on the Roman road to Wroxeter.

\*   \*   \*   \*

Portskewett, on the Severn estuary, was described in the Welsh triads as one of the 3 principal harbors of Wales, a reminder that its importance lay in being the terminus of the ferry across the channel. The main Roman route to the coastal plains of South Wales crossed here from Avonmouth and the railroad ran a steam ferry to Black Rock, where there had been a ferry across the Severn from time immemorial. From Black Rock can be seen the Shoots, a channel ¼ mile wide through which the water rushes madly at ebb tide. Even at low tide there is a depth of 50 feet here. Portskewett village began 5000 years ago, when a great barrow or cairn 70 feet long was set up on Heston Brake, a wooded hilltop with a view across the water. Some stones which formed part of the rooms inside the cairn can still be seen. The entrance opens towards the east between 2 big boulders, one of which is some 6 feet high. This cairn was excavated in 1888 and in a corner of the first room.

Two upright stones here have holes curiously cut in them.

On top of Portskewett Hill are foundations of a Roman building. Here were found coins from Claudius Gothicus to Valens. The ruins suggest that some of the iron workings on the slopes of the hill may be of Roman origin. Down by the waterside is Sudbury Camp. Green grass grows over it, and the Bristol Channel beats against the rocks at the base of the cliff, wearing away the camp year by year. The earthwork was excavated in 1934 to 1936 and was found to have been built by Iron Age people in the 1st Century B. C. It was occupied continuously until about 100 A. D., when the inhabitants were probably moved to the new Roman town of Caerwent. Iron, glass and bronze objects were made here, and a bit of clay crucible with fused bronze attached. In the National Museum at Cardiff can be seen knives, nails, bronze brooches, iron tweezers, beads, and pottery spindle from the site.

\* \* \* \*

Kemeys Inferior is in the quiet valley of the Usk, backed by a wood on the steep slope of the hill. The 13th Century church is perched on a little precipice over the Usk, which can be heard rushing over the stones. The hill is bright with bluebells in the spring.

Llandegveth is on the Soar Brook about 4 miles north of Caerleon. Here St. Tegwedd was martyred by pagan Saxons. She was the mother of St. Teilo.

Llangibby is set amid the beauty of the Usk where St. Cybi built one of 2 churches he built near Caerleon. The summit of Llangibby's tree-clad hill has proved to be near impregnable. In season it is aglow with purple foxgloves.

Llangoven lies hidden in the hills a few miles SE of Raglan. There is a church bearing a gowned figure of St. Govan, a 5th Century Welsh queen and wife of St. Tewdric.

Llansantffraed lies by the red-banked river Usk, the level grass studded with trees, and the wooded hills and mountains in the distance. It is 10 or 12 miles north of Caerleon.

(-not in these notes or this source....it includes the village of Llanon, where St. David is said to have spent his childhood years....)

Gwernesney is a tiny place on the Usk-Chepstow road with a name derived from its alder trees.

\* \* \* \*

Tredunnock was until the early years of the 1800s completely off the beaten track. Then David Edwards, the famous bridge builder, built the narrow stone Newbridge across the Usk, at the spot where it ceases to be tidal. Today we can admire the valley and the tree-covered slopes of Wentwood and watch the cattle as they come down to drink. Attached to the wall of the name of the church is a sandstone memorial with Latin inscription to Julius Julianus.

Bassaleg is now one of Newport's best suburbs, but it has 2 possessions that were here when Newport was a swamp. They are the Gaer Camp and Tredegar Fort, with 3 lines of bank and ditch, finely situated on high ground. Below flows the River Ebbw.

Shirenewton is a hilltop village situated 500 feet above the Bristol Channel. It has a wide view of all the coast of Somerset from Gloucestershire to Devon. In clear weather the Cotswolds, the Mendips, the Quantocks and Exmoor can all be seen across the water. In a wood to the west of the village is the fine hill fort of Llanmelin, once a busy town of the Silures pulsating with life. Nowadays the great banks and ditches are a somber sight, shaded by yews. Llanmelin consists of a main enclosure of 5 ½ acres and a long narrow annex of 2 acres divided into 3 by internal cross banks and ditches. Camp and annex were both defended by multiple ditches and banks and the inner rampart of the main camp was 17 feet wide at the bases. The main fort was built by Iron Age Celts who came into the district about 200 B. C. At the time of the Roman invasion, about 50 A. D., the entrance to the camp was remodeled and about 25 years later the whole settlement was abandoned, probably in favor of the new town of Caerwent in the plain below.

*    *    *    *

Devauden - Roman coins of Antonius have been found here. The road to Devauden runs by Chepstow Park Wood, 100 acres of the Forestry Commission's Dean Forest National Park, on a sandstone hill over 900 feet high. From the great ridge of cedars are views towards the Severn.

*Notes on Ireland and Other Writings*

\*   \*   \*   \*

Trelleck is a hollow set high among the hills and looks to the tree-topped Trelleck Beacon, 1000 feet high and commanding a glorious view of the Wye Valley. There are 3 menhirs standing in a field to the south of the village. They are respectively about 9, 10 and 14 feet high. Traditionally they commemorate a Saxon victory in these parts, but were probably actually standing there for centuries before.

\*   \*   \*   \*

Undy is a humble village straggling along the edge of Caldicot Level. A curious feature is that it has a far greater acreage of foreshore than dry land. A road leads from the village to a little inlet which is all that remains of the town and harbor of Abergwaitha. It was granted to the monks of Tintern 700 years ago and a century later had been ruincd by the general erosion then becoming common on this side of the Severn.

\*   \*   \*   \*

Lady Park Wood (national nature reserve) - many of its steep slopes have never been completely cleared of trees. There are many natural outcrops of limestone where wild thyme and rock roses grow. Scattered over the reserve are oaks, beeches and yews. Here above the Wye are some remarkable rocks. One called the Suck Stone is estimated to weigh at least 10,000 tons; the celebrated Buckstone just across the border of Gloucestershire would appear as a pebble beside it. It lies in a little clearing above the path, its flat top tipped at an angle to the steep hill. Close by, the path comes to an end at the Hearkening Rock, a great wall of stone with a view across the river to Great Doward Woods. It is said that from here the slightest sound from over the Wye can be heard.

*   *   *   *

Monmouthshire is a land of sharp contrasts; picturesque mountains, like the Sugar Loaf and Blorenge in the north and in the south moors flat and fertile. This is a county of forlorn little castles, relics of unhappy border strife in far-off days, lying hidden and almost forgotten among the hills. The county is predominantly hilly or mountainous, the lofty heights loom boldly on the skyline never far away, and pleasant are the pastoral scenes. About 1/8 of the total area is woodland. The Wye enters the Severn at Chepstowe. The chief river is the Usk.

- End of copy from "Monmouthshire" by Arthur Mee, according to her notes (Abridged Version)

\* \* \* \*

## Notes taken from "Fighting Kings of Wessex" by Baker

It was about the time Offa was reigning in Angeln that the force which set the balls rolling appeared in Europe. The Huns, like the Scythians before them and the Mongols after them, emerged from the eastern steppes and began by shattering the great Gothic realm which Irminric, the patriarch of all European kings, had built up along the Vistula. Fleeing from their foes, the Goths crossed the Danube and took refuge in the Roman Empire.

The fame of the deeds that followed was known in Angeln. When the Roman governors attempted to hoodwink and break up the Goths, the latter revolted and defeated a Roman army at the battle of Hadrianople and burnt the emperor Valens in the house where he had taken refuge. By 400 the Goths, under Alaric, were shouldering their tilted wagons over the Alpine passes and pouring into Italy to begin those campaigns which ended with the sack of Rome. The burial of Alaric, with all of his treasure, was in the bed of the River Busentinus and no enterprising treasure seeker has ever found him or his treasure.

\* \* \* \*

After the defeat of the expedition of 407 Britain was never re-garrisoned. The cities of Britain were notified that they must look after themselves. The sack of Rome was serious, but the abandonment of Britain was more serious still, for it unpinned the northern defenses of the empire. The drive of the Huns was pushing all of the fighting tribes of central Europe in a struggling mass upon the Rhine. They burst through in 405 under the leadership of Radagaisus, only to leave their bones in Italy. The Vandals and the Burgundians were next forced through the gap and the civilized land of Gaul was overrun. Attila,

*Notes on Ireland and Other Writings*

on accession, seemed likely to swallow all of Europe. In 451 he crossed the Rhine. The storm burst at Chalons, where on the Catalaunian Plains he was met and beaten by the combined Roman and Gothic armies.

The Franks had been extending their rule over the neighboring country. Their task was to hold the domination so acquired. Whether or not they were aware that possession of the Rhine depended on the attitude of Britain, they made their first step just after the battle of Chalons, to isolate Britain and get it in the safekeeping of their friends.

\*   \*   \*   \*

Vortimer's death threw power back into Vortigern's hands. It was accordingly possible for Hengist to enter into negotiations. He seems to have been the initiating party of the Peace Conference. The conference broke up in disorder. The Franks had so much the best of it that 300 of the British leaders are said to have fallen. The charge is definitely made that Hengist planned a massacre and not only made the British drunk as a precaution, but actually gave a pre-arranged signal. Geoffrey of Monmouth goes into details and tells us of Eldol, the dux of Gloucester, who armed with a stake fought his way successfully out of the Peace Conference. The Anglo-Saxon Chronicle preserves a dignified silence about it.

Vortigern was spared. He purchased his freedom by ceding the 3 provinces which are now Essex, Middlesex and Sussex. The fate of Vortigern is tragic enough. Abandoned by his friends and hated by his people, he wandered about seeking a refuge until, brokenhearted, he met his end.

The fall and death of Vortigern opened a fresh, dramatic chapter in the struggle for Britain. Ambrosius Aurelianus entered the war, and Aelle was fetched to meet him. It is clear that Vortimer had not driven the invaders into their ships. Hengist had carried fire and sword from one end of Britain to the other: a process which was not stayed until, after devastating town and country, it reached the other side of the Island. But it is equally certain that Hengist had not established himself in any part of Britain save Kent. That keen and successful businessman acted with an astuteness which has received less commendation than might have been expected. Kent, from its relation to the continent, had always been

*Notes on Ireland and Other Writings*

the richest part of Britain and the customs barrier of its foreign trade. Hengist proceeded to make himself safe by transferring the task of conquering Britain to broader shoulders than his own.

The grant of something like a legal title to Essex, Middlesex and Sussex furnished him with valuable assets. He was in a position to supply any new partners, not only with such portions of Britain, but with information which would enable them to make good by military means any claim they chose to advance to the rest. The secret of Britain was the secret of the Roman roads.

Notation......we must carefully distinguish between the idea of the English settling along the rivers (which is true) and the idea of their conquering Britain by sailing up the rivers (which is a flat impossibility.) Britain could only have been conquered by properly organized military action along the roads. Anyone who has walked up the Thames beyond Kingston, or the Stour or Avon above Christchurch, will know how impossible it would be to force such avenues against any serious defense.

Hengist had been many years in Britain and traversed most of it, either as a friend or as a foe. He was therefore quite aware of those facts respecting the course of the Roman roads and the position of the road junctions, ignorance of which for 50 years prevented the Danes later on from successfully invading Britain. No trace survives of the negotiations or when the transfer was made but with the arrival of Aelle, the conquest passed out of the stage of private enterprise into royal hands, so the English kings must have arrived at the same time or shortly before.

Ambrosius Aurelianus was the refuge to which all the British turned, as chickens to a hen, and his wings were wide. It was the year in which Count Ricimer was assassinated at Rome; and perhaps the rise of Ambrosius – himself Roman by descent – was one of the results of that wave of anti-Germanism.

But 5 years were to pass and then the return blow came. In 476 Odovacar the Rugian overthrew the last Roman emperor of the west, Romulus Augustulus, and became king of Italy. In the year following Aelle arrived. It may be true as the Anglo-Saxon Chronicle says, that Aelle and his sons arrived in 3 ships, but we may take it that far more than 3 followed and preceded him. The conquest had now begun in earnest.

The distribution of the English king-
doms in later times gives us a hint of Aelle's
strategy. For the English to advance westward from Kent presented difficulties. The
great forest of Anderida, running right up
northwest, created a bottleneck between
woods and the river Thames in the wild
heaths and marshes beyond Kingston.
The very few routes westward were easily
defensible. The only great Roman road ran
to London. There may have been some con-
nection between these facts and the difficulty with Hengist making himself master
of Britain. So they adopted another plan
and Aelle seems to have followed a variant
of the same strategy.

Essex was an early and certainly important English kingdom. It included probably most of Middlesex and Hertfordshire
with London, and extending south over
the river into Surrey. How far it reached
to the north is unknown. From Colchester
in this territory the Roman roads were still
in good condition and ran west, north and
south. It was a strategic center. By these
roads armies could capture London, cross
the river southward and link up with the
English on the Sussex coast.

Aelle's chief attack went through
Colchester and penetrated toward the Trent

*Notes on Ireland and Other Writings*

valley. It was commanded by the king of Angeln, the Icel who appears in the genealogies. Icel was then to turn south and press towards Gloucester and Cirencester and the Thames valley. The occupation of East Anglia would be an incident in this great scheme...and the establishment of the kingdom of Essex would have included the capture of London, the acquisition of Surrey from the north and access to the Roman road (Stane Street) which led down to Chichester.

We know from the Anglo-Saxon Chronicle that Aelle himself undertook the task of reducing the southern portion of the Saxon shore that stretched along the coast of Sussex. His object in capturing Anderida Forest was for the iron mines. This district had a certain independence of its own. Its seaport was for many years one of the chief seaports of England. His turning movement around the great forest would give him the narrow coastal strip that reaches to Chichester and Portchester: the forest still lay impenetrable. It was this part of the plan, that he conducted in person, that went awry. No more has come down to us of the campaigns of Icel, king of Angeln. We only know that he successfully carried out his own part of the work.

Footnote: (If Aelle had succeeded, his "Sussex" would have comprised the whole of England south of the Thames save Kent....the Wessex of Ina, but not the Wessex of Egbert. It was not in Hengist's interest that Aelle succeed too well.)

About Aelle's part which met with disaster, if Portchester was not seized its capture was surely intended. The Jutes seized the Isle of Wight and reached the Hampshire coast as far as the Avon. Then something went very seriously wrong, and they never got any further. They had in the Isle of Wight the point of access to southwest Britain – if they could have won it, Ambrosius would have been nipped between the armies of Aelle and the armies of Icel coming from the north. But no such event came to pass. The forest still cut them off, and they could not win through to the inland districts. They must have been repulsed along the line from Portchester and Winchester, and they never reached the great road-junctions of Axminster and Dorchester.

Footnote: It seems just possible that Aelle had erroneous information and was looking for Axminster in the wrong neighborhood. The correct position of Axminster is also exactly the kind of point of which Hengist

*Notes on Ireland and Other Writings*

might have been ignorant, for pursuit of Picts and Scots would never have taken him there.

British sources tell us of the 12 great battles of Ambrosius, and they seem to have been no myth. The Anglo-Saxon Chronicles claim 2 victories for Aelle. Even today at Pevensey in Sussex the huge walls of the Roman citadel stand stark and bare as Aelle left them. The war culminated in a crushing defeat of the English at Mount Badon. Hengist died in 488, for in that year his son silently succeeds to the kingdom of Kent. Aelle, after 491, silently vanishes out of history. He had failed, and his countrymen covered up his failure with a profound silence which 15 centuries have not broken. We do not know when he died, or where or how, nor his kinship. His name is not included in the royal genealogies of the English. His repute survived in a curious, haunting way. We can guess that he was a great man, for he ruled all of the English; and the silence that covers him is as great as he was.

- End of copy from "Fighting Kings of Wessex" by Baker, according to her notes (Abridged Version)

*   *   *   *

## Notes taken from "Everyday Life in Anglo-Saxon, Viking and Norman Times" by Quennell

The Saxons adorned themselves with fine barbaric necklaces – big lumps of garnet, amber, crystal, amethyst or beads of glass colored in many ways. The brooches used to fasten the cloak can be traced back to the Goths in S. Russia and from the Baltic coast and Scandinavia.

Horses were decked out as beautifully as their masters.

*   *   *   *

Anglo-Saxon military man: He wore a shirt and breeches, sometimes cut off at the knee, when hose like leggings were worn, and fastened by cross garters which were part of the leather shoes. Over the shirt a tunic or coat, with long sleeves tight at the wrist where the sleeves were fastened with metal clasps. This coat was belted at the waist. His helmet had an iron frame, filled in between with horn. It had a boar on the crest. His cloak was fastened on breast or shoulder with a brooch.

*Notes on Ireland and Other Writings*

The spear was the commonest weapon in the early pagan days. The shaft was of ash, 6 to7 feet long, and some were thrown as javelins. The early swords were formidable weapons a yard long and the later types had a tapered blade. Battle axes were used, and some were thrown.

- End of these notes (Abridged Version)

\*    \*    \*    \*

## Notes taken from "Everyday Life in Roman Britain" by Quennell

The battles of the empire were won by the Legionary, who threw his javelin, then rushed into close quarters and fought with his short sword which was a cut and thrust weapon.

The Auxilliaries were divided into infantry cohorts of 500 to 1000 strong, and cavalry troops. They were commanded by Roman officers, and while their pay was less than the Legionary's, their service was longer. They received Roman citizenship on discharge.

An auxilliary cavalryman wore only a leather jerkin, without body armor, an oval shield, and a longer sword.

*Notes on Ireland and Other Writings*

The pilum (javelin) of the Legionary had an iron head fixed onto a wooden shaft, and the weight of the iron head kept the javelin in a straight line when it was thrown. We do not know what the range of the pilum was.

\*    \*    \*    \*

The Roman forts were provided with sufficient corn for a year, so they could withstand siege.

All cooking was done on a raised hearth made of masonry. The charcoal fuel was kept in the arch below. The fire was on this open hearth, and the dangerous charcoal fumes must have been carried away by a hood over the hearth into a wall flue.

\*    \*    \*    \*

The monastery was to become the one place where a man could do quiet work, and the cloak of religion the only substitute for a sharp sword.

- End of these notes (Abridged Version)

\*    \*    \*    \*

## Notes taken from "London Through the Ages" by Stuart

The Caesars died out with Nero....Later emperors still called themselves 'Caesar' but they had no hereditary claim, but were chosen and acclaimed by the army. Presently various legions in various places began to choose Caesars of their own. There were as many as five emperors minting their own coinage at one period – with the result that for a strong central authority, defense against barbarian invaders was difficult if not impossible to organize.

Savage tribes from central and eastern Europe poured into the rich plains of Italy. Scots and Picts invaded Britain from the north, Saxon pirates poured upon the coasts of Britain and Gaul; the first shadow of the Dark Ages was creeping over Europe.

From 287 to 293 Britain had a Caesar of her own, Carausius, a curly-haired sea pilot from the land now called Belgium. He came with a large band of followers, and caused himself to be proclaimed emperor. He minted gold and silver coins bearing his head and he began to build a navy; then he was murdered by another would-be Caesar, the despicable Allectus, whose reign was even more brief. The great war

*Notes on Ireland and Other Writings*

galley discovered in 1910 in deep mud at the southern end of Westminster Bridge was probably a unit in the fleet of one or other of these upstart Caesars.

It happened that one of the associate emperors far away in Italy was a man of strong character. His name was Flavius Constantius Chlorus. In the year 292 he landed in Britain, defeated Allectus and was joyfully welcomed by the Londoners. In honor of this event a gold medal was struck, and it is here that London comes into the picture again. Through a turreted gate rides Constantius, spear in hand; to greet him kneels a woman with arms upraised.

Constantius took energetic measure for the defense of Britain, threatened by blue-painted Picts as well as by red-haired Saxon pirates. It was his son, Constantine the Great, who by making Christianity the official religion of the Roman Empire changed the whole course of history. The new religion spread slowly in Londinium. In 303 A. D. a Roman soldier, Albanus by name, was beheaded within 20 miles of the city for befriending a fugitive Christian priest from Wales.

- End of these notes (Abridged Version)

*Notes on Ireland and Other Writings*

\*   \*   \*   \*

It was to defend Italy against the Goths that Rome in the opening of the 5th Century withdrew her legions from Britain, and from that moment the struggle was unaided against the Picts, marauding Irish (at that time called Scots) and Saxon pirates. For 40 years Britain held out bravely against these assailants, but civil strife broke its powers of resistance.

In 491 Pevensey fell to the enemy and the kingdom of the South Saxons was established.

(Notes taken from Green's "History of the English People," Book I)............abridged version of the notes

\*   \*   \*   \*

Check "The Yeoman's England" by Thomas for information on bees and other rural and wildlife in England

\*   \*   \*   \*

St. Elaeth - a 6th Century saint and poet, who before he took to a saintly life, had been a king in a district in the north of England.

Theodosius - in 369 he arrived and put a stop to the devastation of the Saxons and tribesmen.

King Arthur - according to Nennius, Arthur was King or Duke of the Britons and his activity manifested itself in all parts of the country. In Welsh he is called Amherawdyr (Emperor) but not king till late.

- notes taken from "The Welsh People" (abridged version of notes)

\*     \*     \*     \*

Cotswold Hills - part of a limestone ridge which crosses England from SW to NE, characterized by more rugged scenery than that of the chalk ridges; valleys, often steep-sided, are generally wooded but uplands are grassy or heathery.

Bristol - where the Avon has cut a gorge through a branch of the Mendip hills.

Cheddar - limestone gorge and caves.

Herefordshire - a Welsh border county with deep red soil.

Usk river - border river between England and Wales.

(- notes taken from "A Pictorial Atlas of the British Isles" - abridged version of notes)

*   *   *   *

Glastonbury Tor was only 500 feet high, but seemed much higher because it rose so sharply from the flat country around it.
Cheddar Gorge winding up into the hills - was like some fantastic canyon out of a western film - sheer gray crags soared skyward.

(notes taken from "The Young Traveler in England and Wales" - abridged version of notes)

*   *   *   *

## Notes taken from "The Boyne and the Blackwater" by Wilde

The plains of Midhe (Meath), and the flowery fields of Bregha, through which the Boyne flows.......

The first fortified houses and stone buildings that we read of were in Meath.

.....about the middle or toward the end of the 2nd Century Tuathal Teachtmar, one of the pagan monarchs, ruled at Tara and he erected Meath into a 5th province by taking in portions of the other four; hence the Irish historians derived its name of Midhe – a neck – on account of its being formed by necks taken from the surrounding provinces.

\*     \*     \*     \*

.....one of our oldest coins is of Aedh, King of Meath.

There were 4 royal palaces of great celebrity in Meath in ancient times.

\*     \*     \*     \*

The Boyne rises in the barony and near the little village of Carbury in county Kildare, about 7 miles SE of Enfield and 4 miles from Edenderry. Running westward for a few miles, it reaches Offaly county and then becomes the boundary between counties, draining in its course the surplus waters of the adjacent great Bog of Allen. Leaving Offaly county upon its NW bank, it touches Meath near Castle-Jordan and forms the boundary between that county and Kildare, until it reaches Ashford, below the bridge of Clonard. In this portion of its course it receives the Yellow River and Milltown stream. From Ashford to a few miles above Drogheda it traverses the fertile plains of Meath.

After passing Trim and then Navan, it receives the Blackwater from Cavan, which there is almost as large as the Boyne itself. The Boyne measures about 70 miles in its windings. From its source through Offaly county the Boyne is an insignificant stream, as in Kildare. In Kildare it flows its tortuous course through marshy country and is constantly broken with islands. It flows through this type of country in upper Meath also.

Three great natural divisions present themselves to the topographer of the Boyne: first, from its source to Clonard; second, Clonard to Navan; and third, from

*Notes on Ireland and Other Writings*

Navan to the sea; each presenting a character peculiar to itself.

Near Clonard, upon the SE shore of the Boyne, is a circular earthen fort of the military class, belonging to the times before stone buildings were much in use.

These ancient forts contain a central subterranean chamber, and circular passages probably for security reasons, and to serve as granaries. Weapons, ornaments and animal remains have been found in and around these enclosures.

\*   \*   \*   \*

The 2nd great division of the Boyne extends from Clonard to Navan. In the first portion of this division, from Clonard to Trim, a distance of about 10 miles, the river's character varies little from the previous descriptions; slow, deep and tortuous it winds on its placid course through deep, alluvial meadows, to the bridge of Stonyford, over which the road from Mullingar to Trim crosses to the southern bank. For the next 4 miles of its course there is little to attract attention; the banks are low and the country very flat, and liable to yearly inundations.

The fish of the Boyne have been celebrated in ancient story, which we have reason to believe were salmon.

The next bridge we meet is near where the Kildare Blackwater empties itself, and beyond it that of Scariff, below which the river is broken into a great number of islands, and intersected by weirs. The road approaches to within a few yards of the stream at this point, and here the true sylvan beauty of the Boyne commences. The surrounding country now is light in soil and used chiefly as meadow and pasture land, due to the yearly inundations.

Passing down the river from Newtown – Trim, its banks assume a more elevated and broken appearance – now swelling gradually into long, undulating mounds and depressing into broad meadows, and the stream itself quickens its course and its waters assume a brighter appearance, but still dotted with islands, as in its previous portions of its course.

The next point of beauty is Rathnally, where the banks rise on both sides to a considerable elevation – noble trees, the deep sullen waters of the river, the calm stillness of the scene, the long dark vistas through which the stream winds – form the charming landscape.

From Becture Abbey, founded in the middle of the 12th Century, to Navan, the Boyne sweeps through banks not high or abrupt, but of gentle undulations of surface and pleasing slopes.

Several subterranean chambers and passages, some of them similarly constructed, exist in Connacht and Munster. They are generally formed in the raised embankment or within the precincts of an ancient fort. The peasants believe they were built by the Danes, though with no authority.

Passing through Bellinter, the Boyne is again broken into islands. Turning south from Bellinter Bridge,we begin to ascend the hill of Tara.....retracing our steps for a short way from Riverstown, we meet a ruined fortress and now we commence the ascent of Tara by the ancient road leading to the north, the Slope of the Chariots.

Crossing the Boyne once more at Bellinter Bridge, in no part of the course does the river present the extreme calmness as here. Widening into deep,still pools, shaded by aged timber and fringed with wild plants of gigantic growth, blue forget-me-nots, yellow potentillas peeping through the foliage, and water lilies. Lime trees, grey-stemmed beeches and ancient yew trees abound here.

The Boyne now turns north toward Navan. A road leads from Bellinter to Navan along the left bank of the Boyne. At Kilcarn, immediately adjoining Cannistown, the Dublin road is carried over the Boyne by a well-built bridge and continues upon the western bank, between which the river intervenes. The opposite bank rises abruptly from the waters' edge and forms a wooded rampart from this point to Navan.

At Navan just below the bridge which crosses it on the Drogheda road, the Boyne receives the Blackwater, which at this point is nearly as large as the Boyne.

The Blackwater runs out of Loch Ramor, in SE County Cavan. Its entire length in all its windings is about 20 miles and flows from NW to SE. The great northern road from Navan to Virginia, through Kells, passes first upon its northern bank and then upon its southern bank for its entire course.

Loch Ramor is charmingly irregular, and studded with islands. The lake is about 5 miles long and 1 to 1 ½ miles wide.

After a course of about 1 ½ miles the river touches Meath at the barony of Castlekieran. Completely entering Meath,

*Notes on Ireland and Other Writings*

for the first few miles it passes a number of forts, which crowd upon both sides of the river and show this district's military importance in early times.

The Blackwater now winds towards Kells, and to the SW the beautiful hill of Lloyd. The river then bends somewhat to the south, and in the region of Headford spreads out into a series of small lakes and ponds, partly natural and partly artificial. Within ¾ of a mile to the SW of the river stands Kells.

Descending the river upon the northern bank we arrive at Teltown, about midway between Kells and Navan. Upon a green hill sloping gradually from the waters' edge, and rising to a height of about 200 feet, may be seen a large earthen fort. About a furlong's length to the right of the road, with a few hollows or excavations in the adjoining lands, apparently the sites of small dried-up lakes; and to the left of the road, parts of the trench and embankment of 2 other forts, which must have been of immense size, greater even than those existing now at Tara. These mark the site of the early pagan settlement.

Standing in the center of this fort and looking up towards the northwest, the hill of Lloyd presents a grand and imposing object; in the extreme distance we see the rounded hills of Cavan bound the horizon; and following its track by the little ruined church at Teltown, the heights of Donaghpatrick, and over the woods of Liscarton, the eye rests upon the hills of Skreen and Tara in the extreme NE.

We now reach Donaghpatrick and the church there, one of the earliest sacred stone edifices erected in Ireland after the introduction of Christianity.

From hence to Navan objects of almost equal interest present themselves on both sides of the Blackwater. The scenery is the same with graceful, well-wooded, swelling undulations. Upon the SW bank we have the fine moat of Navan, about 1 1/2miles lower down from Liscarton Castle. This moat of Navan is of the military class and forms a conspicuous object from all sides, because of its size and its appearing to have been formed in part out of the natural hill.

From Navan to the Boyne's mouth, though intersected by several weirs and descending several rapids, has been rendered navigable by means of a canal. Adjoining the region of Blackcastle on the Slane road about a mile from Navan, on the west bank of the Boyne we pass the round tower and church of Donaghmore. The original church was called the great church of the plain of Echnach, and is said to owe its origin to St. Patrick.

Next we come to Ardmulchan church on the right bank, and somewhat below it, Dunmore castle on the left bank. Here are high crags, steep precipitous banks, Rhine-like scenery. Dunmore castle stands on a commanding eminence, above one of the fords of the Boyne.

Below Beauparc we pass Slane Castle. Then still on the northern bank, we see the church or hermitage of St. Erc in a grove of ancient yew trees, down on the shore immediately below Slane Castle.

Erc was the first bishop of Slane, consecrated by St. Patrick and died A. D. 514. He was Patrick's judge. St. Erc disobeyed the Druid's injunction and stood up to honor Patrick, and receiving Patrick's blessing, became a believer.

\*     \*     \*     \*

Newgrange is an enormous cairn of small stones calculated at 180,000 tons of weight, and occupies the summit of one of the natural undulating slopes which enclose the Boyne valley upon the north.

It is said to cover nearly 2 acres and is 4oo paces around, and now about 50 feet higher than the adjoining natural surface. Various excavations made in its sides and summit at different times have lessened its original height. It is overgrown mostly with hazel. A few yards from the outer circle of the mound, there appears to have stood originally a circle of enormous detached blocks of stone, placed at intervals of about 10 yards from each other. It is said that a large pillar once stood upon its summit. This mound is hollow. It contains a large chamber, formed by enormous stones and is accessible through a narrow passage, also formed of huge stones placed together without mortar or cement. Some of these rocks both inside and out bear marks of being water-worn, and were probably lifted from the bed of the Boyne. Others belong to a class of rock not founding the neighborhood at all; some are basaltic and others must have been transported from the Mourne Mts....the entrance of the mound is nearly square.

Within view of Newgrange and about a mile distant, seated on one of the higher slopes of the Boyne's bank is Dowth, the 3rd great cone of the group. Not as broad at the base as Newgrange, it is more conical. A

circle of boulder-like stones originally surrounded the base of this mound, which is
formed entirely of small, loose stones. The
external surface, however, has been covered with a thick and verdant sod. During
the excavations at Dowth some interesting
relics and antiques were found.

Below Dowth the banks in many places
rise high and abrupt from the water's edge.
Near Oldbridge, where the Mattock river
enters the Boyne, it is again possible to
travel along the river bank.

The first rapid on the Boyne occurs at
the Boyne obelisk, built to commemorate
the passage of the Boyne when Stuart and
Nassau contended for the crown of those
realms.

After the Boyne passes the great mon-
ument of Newgrange it alters its course,
turning north, and with various minor
windings forms a deep curve between
that point and Drogheda, which is about
5 miles distant. Reaching Townley Hall it
again turns SE towards Drogheda. Within
this bend of the river, upon the right or
south bank, the ground rises by a succession of smooth and gentle slopes to the conspicuous hill of Donore. The Boyne winds
round in front of this hill to the north.

*Notes on Ireland and Other Writings*

Immediately behind it, towards the south, the way lies open to Dublin. To the extreme NW lies Slane, about 9 miles from Drogheda following the windings of the river.

Some weirs, about ½ mile below Slane, point out the site of ancient fords. Above the entrance of the Mattock river, the Boyne is fordable with difficulty, and the right bank rises rather precipitously immediately beyond its margin. The river then turns SW and just below the obelisk it enlarges considerably, and several islands occur in it – the most extensive being Grove Island and Yellow Island. The shallowest ford occurs here; an old road leads down to it and it is passable for carriage and horses at low water in summertime.

\*　\*　\*　\*

On the high bank above and to the east of this valley was placed King William's chief battery. William and his army marched in 2 columns from Ardee. Having arrived within view of Drogheda the position of the Irish camp stretching along the slopes of the hill of Donore was at once recognized. A person standing on any of the elevations in the vicinity could with ease recognize every tent in the Irish camp.

Eastward of the King's Glen, in the same hill, was another deep narrow ravine, very similar to the King's Glen.

*   *   *   *

Duleek is a long, straggling village 4 miles from Drogheda and 3 miles from Donore. Historic authorities say that St. Patrick erected a church here and placed over it St. Cianan, whom he had baptized and adopted as his own son, and to whom he bequeathed his own copy of the Gospels. Before St. Cianan's time the churches of Ireland were built of wattles or boards and not stone.

A bluff hill rises behind Duleek to the southeast. The little hamlet of the Naul is placed in a deep gorge, through which the streamlet Delvin flows. This stream divides the counties of Meath and Dublin. From Duleek to this point the road stretches along the sides of the succession of hills which lead up to Bellewstown. The Black Castle of the Naul stands on a gray perpendicular rock that rises abruptly out of a most romantic little dell through which the rivulet meanders.

*Notes on Ireland and Other Writings*

\*　\*　\*　\*

The Irish name of Drogheda is the Bridge of the Ford.

Below Drogheda, the Boyne spreads out in a broad estuary.

St. Patrick landed at the mouth of the Boyne in 432, on the southern bank.

(End of notes from "The Boyne and the Blackwater" by Wilde, according to her notes - abridged version of notes used)

\*　\*　\*　\*

# FAVORITE POEMS

(With some of these, I wonder if the spelling and punctuation are how the poet had it....I am writing from the copies my aunt had....hopefully they are correct.)

## Stopping By Woods on a
## Snowy Evening

Whose woods these are I think I know.
His house is in the village though;
He will not see me stopping here
To watch his woods fill up with snow.

My little horse must think it queer
To stop without a farmhouse near
Between the woods and frozen lake
The darkest evening of the year.

He gives his harness bells a shake
To ask if there is some mistake.
The only other sounds the sweep
Of easy wind and downy flake.

The woods are lovely dark and deep
But I have promises to keep,
And miles to go before I sleep,
And miles to go before I sleep.

By Robert Frost

*Notes on Ireland and Other Writings*

## Alec Speaking

He is putting it lithely when he says
Quobble in the Grass,
Strab he down the soddieflays
Amo amat amass;
Amonk amink aminibus,
Amarmylaidie Moon,
Amikky mendip multiplus
Amighty midgey spoon.
And so I traddled onward
Careing not a care
Onward, Onward, Onward.
Onward, my friends to victory and glory
For the thirtyninth.

By John Lennon

## Ars Poetica

A poem should be palpable and mute
As a globed fruit

Dumb
As old medallions to the thumb

Silent as the sleeve-worn stone
Of casement ledges where the moss has
grown

A poem should be wordless
As the flight of birds

A poem should be motionless in time
As the moon climbs
Leaving, as the moon behind the winter
leaves,
Memory by memory the mind
A poem should be motionless in time as
the moon climbs

A poem should be equal to:
Not true

For all the history of grief
An empty doorway and a maple leaf

*Notes on Ireland and Other Writings*

For love
The leaning grasses and two lights above
the sea

A poem should not mean
But be.

By Archibald MacLeish

*Notes on Ireland and Other Writings*

## When You Are Old

When you are old and grey and full of
sleep,
And nodding by the fire, take down this
book,
And slowly read, and dream of the soft
look
Your eyes had once, and of their shadows
deep;

How many loved your moments of glad
grace,
And loved your beauty with love false or
true,
But one man loved the pilgrim soul in
you,
And loved the sorrows of your changing
face;

And bending down beside the glowing
kars,
Murmur, a little sadly, how love fled
And paced upon the mountains overhead
And hid his face amid a crowd of stars.

By W. B. Yeats

*Notes on Ireland and Other Writings*

## From The Sensitive Plant

Whether the sensitive plant, or that
Which within its boughs like a Spirit sat,
Ere its outward form had known decay,
Now felt this change, I cannot say.

Whether that Lady's gentle mind,
No longer with the form combined
Which scatters love, as stars do light,
Found sadness, where it left delight,

I dare not guess: but in this life
Of error, ignorance, and strife,
Where nothing is, but all things seem,
And we the shadows of the dream,

It is a modest creed, and yet
Pleasant if one considers it,
To own that death itself must be,
Like all the rest, a mockery.

That garden sweet, that lady fair,
And all sweet shapes and odours there,
In truth have never passed away:
'Tis we, 'Tis we, are changed; not they.

*Notes on Ireland and Other Writings*

For love, and beauty, and delight,
There is no death nor change: their might
Exceeds our organs, which endure
No light, being themselves obscure.

Shelley.....1820

*Notes on Ireland and Other Writings*

## From A Defence of Poetry

......"Reason is the enumeration of quantities already known; imagination is the perception of the value of those quantities.."

".....Sounds as well as thoughts have relation both between each other and towards that which they represent...."

"Poetry....awakens and enlarges the mind itself by rendering it the receptacle of a thousand unapprehended combinations of thoughts..."

The great instrument of moral good is the imagination; and poetry administers to the effect by acting upon the cause..."

"When corruption avails so as to extinguish in them the sensibility to pleasure, passion, and natural scenery, which is imputed to them as an imperfection, the last triumph of evil will have been achieved."

Poetic principle has led to "....The abolition of personal slavery, and the emancipation of women from a great part of the

*Notes on Ireland and Other Writings*

degrading restraints of antiquity, were among the consequences of these events."

"...We have more moral, political, and historical wisdom, than we know how to reduce into practice; we have more scientific and economical knowledge than can be accommodated to the just distribution of the produce which it multiplies. The poetry in these systems of thought, is concealed by the accumulation of facts and calculating processes."

By Shelley

*Notes on Ireland and Other Writings*

## To A Sky-Lark

Hail, to thee blithe spirit!
Bird thou never wert,
That from heaven, or near it,
Pourest thy full heart
In profuse strains of unpremeditated art.

Higher still, and higher,
From the earth thou springest,
Like a cloud of fire;
The blue deep thou wingest,
And singing still dost soar, and soaring
ever singest.

In the golden lightning
Of the setting sun,
O'er which clouds are brightening,
Thou dost float and run,
Like an unbodied joy whose race is just
begun.

The pale purple even
Melts around thy flight;
Like a star of heaven,
In the broad day light
Thou art unseen, but yet I hear thy shrill
delight.

Keen as are the arrows
Of that silver sphere,
Whose intense lamp narrows
In the white dawn clear,
Until we hardly see, we feel that it is
there.

All the earth and air
With thy voice is loud;
As, when night is bare,
From one lonely cloud
The moon rains out her beams, and
heaven is overflowed.

What thou art we know not;
What is most like thee?
From rainbow clouds there flow not
Drops so bright to see,
As from thy presence showers a rain of
melody.

Like a poet hidden
In the light of thought,
Singing hymns unbidden,
Till the world is wrought
To sympathy with hopes and fears it
heeded not.

Like a high-born maiden
In a palace tower,
Soothing her love-laden
Soul in secret hour
With music sweet as love, which over-
flows her bower.

Like a glow worm golden
In a dell of dew
Scattering unbeholden
Its aerial hue
Among the flowers and grass, which
screen it from the view.

Like a rose embowered
In its own green leaves,
By warm winds deflowered,
Till the sent gives
Makes faint with too much sweet these
heavy-winged thieves.

What objects are the fountains
Of thy happy strain?
What fields, or waves, or mountains?
What shapes of sky or plain?
What love of thine own kind? What igno-
rance of pain?

With thy clear keen joyance
Languor cannot be;
Shadow of annoyance
Never came near thee:
Thou lovest; but ne'er knew love's sad
satiety.

Waking or asleep,
Thou of death must deem
Things more true and deep
Than we mortals dream,
Or how could thy notes flow in such a
crystal stream?

We look before and after,
And pine for what is not:
Our sincerest laughter
With some pain is frought;
Our sweetest songs are those that tell of
saddest thought.

Yet if we could scorn
Hate, and pride, and fear;
If we were things born
Not to shed a tear,
I know not how thy joy we ever should
come near.

*Notes on Ireland and Other Writings*

Better than all measures
Of delightful sound,
Better than all treasures
That in books are found,
Thy skill to poet were, thou scourner of
the ground.

Teach me half the gladness
That thy brain must know,
Such harmonious madness
From my lips would flow,
The world would listen then, as I am lis-
tening now.

By Shelley.....circa 1825

*Notes on Ireland and Other Writings*

## Excerpts from Walt Whitman - Leaves of Grass

The Commonplace

The commonplace I sing;
How cheap is health! how cheap nobility!
Abstinence, no falsehood, no gluttony,
lust;
The open air I sing, freedom, toleration,
(Take here the mainest lesson- less from
books- less from the schools,)
The common day and night- the common
earth and waters,
Your farm- your work- trade, occupation,
The democratic wisdom underneath, like
solid ground for all.


Unseen Buds

Unseen buds, infinite, hidden well,
Under the snow and ice, under the darkness, in every square or cubic inch,
Germinal, exquisite, in delicate lace,
microscopic, unborn,
Like babies in wombs, latent, folded,
compact, sleeping;

*Notes on Ireland and Other Writings*

Billions of billions, and trillions of trillions of them waiting
(On the earth and in the sea- the uni-
verse- the stars there in the heavens,)
Urging slowly, surely forward, forming
endless,
And waiting ever more, forever more
behind.

*Notes on Ireland and Other Writings*

## Auguries of Innocence

To see a World in a grain of Sand
And a Heaven in a wild Flower
Hold Infinity in the palm of your hand
And Eternity in an hour

A Robin Red breast in a cage
Puts all Heaven in a rage
A Dove house filled with doves and
Pigeons
Shudders Hell thro all its regions
A Dog starved at his masters Gate
Predicts the ruin of the state
A horse misused upon the road
Calls to Heaven for Human Blood
Each outcry of the hunted hare
A fibre from the brain does tear
A Skylark wounded in the wing
A Cherubim does cease to sing
The game cock clipd & armd for fight
Does the rising Sun affright
Every Wolf and Lions Howl
Raises from Hell a Human Soul
The wild dear wandering here and there
Keeps the Human Soul From Care
The Lamb misused breeds Public strife
And yet forgives the butchers knife
The bat that flits at close of Eve

*Notes on Ireland and Other Writings*

Has left the brain that wont believe
The Owl that calls upon the Night
Speaks the Unbelievers fright
He who shall hurt the little Wern
Shall never be belovd by men
He who the Ox to wrath has moved
Shall never be by woman lovd
The wanton Boy that kills the fly
Shall feel the spiders Emnity.

By William Blake

*Notes on Ireland and Other Writings*

## THE DUSK OF HORSES

Right under their noses, the green
Of the fields is paling away
Because of something fallen from the sky.

They see this, and put down
Their long heads deeper in grass
That only just escapes reflecting them

As the dream of a millpond would.
The color green flees over the grass
Like an insect, following the red sun over

The next hill. The grass is white.
There is no cloud so dark and white at
once;
There is no pool at dawn that deepens

Their faces and thirsts as this does.
Now they are feeding on solid
Cloud, and, one by one,

With nails as silent as stars among the
wood
Hewed down years ago and now rotten,
The stalls are put up around them.

Now if they lean, they come

*Notes on Ireland and Other Writings*

On wood on any side. Not touching it,
they sleep.
No beast ever lived who understood

What happened among the sun's fields,
Or cared why the color of grass
Fled over the hill while he stumbled,

Led by the halter to sleep
On his four taxed, worthy legs.
Each thinks he awakens where

The sun is black on the rooftop,
That the green is dancing in the next
pasture,
And that the way to sleep

In a cloud, or in a risen lake,
Is to walk as though he were still
In the drained field standing, head down,

To pretend to sleep when led,
And thus to go under the ancient white
Of the meadow, as green goes

And whiteness comes up through his face
Holding stars and rotten rafters,
Quiet, fragrant, and relieved.

By James Dickey

## A Brook in the City

The Farmhouse lingers, though averse to
square
With the new city street it has to wear
A number in. But what about the brook
That held the house as in an
elbow-crook?
I ask as one who knew the brook, its
strength
And impulse, having dipped a finger
length
And made it leap my knuckle, having
tossed
A flower to try its currents where they
crossed.
The meadow grass could be cemented
down
From growing under pavements of a
town;
The apple trees be sent to hearth-stone
flame.
Is water wood to serve a brook the same?
How else dispose of an immortal force
No longer needed? Staunch it at its
source
With cinder loads dumped down? The
brook was thrown
Deep in a sewer dungeon under stone

*Notes on Ireland and Other Writings*

In feted darkness still to live and run-
And all for nothing it had ever done
Except forget to go in fear perhaps.
No one would know except for ancient
maps
That such a brook ran water. But I
wonder
If from its being kept forever under
The thoughts may not have risen that so
keep
This new-built city from both work and
sleep.

By Robert Frost

# NANCY HENNESSY'S POEMS

# The Star-Fish

In the tidal pool a new star-fish
Spirit of adventure burning bright
In his little heart,
Cradled in the sand

Outside, scorching sand
Once, he ventured out there.

Clinging sand and blazing sun
Seared and shriveled his coat
Floundering, teetering
In treacherous stuff

He at last slides back into his element
And gazes out....but never again !!

*Notes on Ireland and Other Writings*

## A Walk on the Beach

Sand, framing the sea;
Eons past, ocean-crushed rock
Spewed up by the tides.
Eternal rhythm,
Hurling up a motley cargo
Seaweed, broken bottles,
Agates, driftwood and shells
Treasure-trove for the children,
To clutch and hoard;
And to dream on.

*Notes on Ireland and Other Writings*

# Cedar

I rest supine athwart the stream
Hidden by the canyon wall
Fern hung, rising towards the sky.
Once I too, reached for the stars,
Stretching, growing to capacity with effort.

A child comes
And spends quiet hours with me.
He has fellowship with the creatures
here.
Frogs are especially drawn to him,
Sitting for hours on his hand.

He talks to them, and says they answer.
Few of his kind would believe this.
He can break his heart over this.
Still, like the cedar he has strength,
And he knows what he knows.

*Notes on Ireland and Other Writings*

## Memories of a Long-Ago December Day

December's pewter sky hurls
The stiletto stabbing at my face
And the mourners beside
My questing, bewildered eyes
Lift to them in mute appeal,
But no answering smile responds.
Tear-filled eyes cannot see my need.

No help there !!

Tearless, benumbed,
I turn back,
Cringing with each thudding impact
Of the insensate clods.

They whisper furtively to each other,
"She will not weep....
She does not care.
She is hard. Hard."

Is the leaden sky weeping for me?
But I am uncaring now.
I have escaped into my fortress
And bolted the door.

*Notes on Ireland and Other Writings*

## Nursing Home Visitor

Come along, old friend.
Shake off those aches and pains.
Step with me through the open door
And your step will be spritely,
Your heart will race once more
With delight of long ago.

The past, forgotten,
Scattered by the wind.
No do not draw back, do not fear.
Just one step more and you can see
Old friends, old loves,
All there, waiting.

*Notes on Ireland and Other Writings*

## Dolphins, Playing

The dolphins drift on the swells,
Pose picturesquely atop the cresting
wave.
Then down, deep, deep into the depths,
And up once more, and alerted
To the good ship 'Wayfarer' peering at
them
Sails shimmering in sunlight over the
horizon

The dolphins drift on the swells,
Pose picturesquely atop the cresting
wave.
Then they're off,
Frolicking, rollicking,
In the foaming wake.

*Notes on Ireland and Other Writings*

## Seven!

Dawn, on the longed-for morning - Seven
today;
I am very mature now, and no longer
protest
The oatmeal for breakfast.

Yesterday, in a shop, I saw a little bicycle,
Bravely red, and my father said,
"Don't you think that is a fine bicycle,"
and smiled at me.

Soon now, after the oatmeal, there will be
the Presents.
There will be a kite; there is always a kite,
To sail gallantly across the sky on gusty
winds.

And *should* there be a bicycle, I will ride,
Ride into my kingdom-world, to see the
great white ships,
Scudding across sun-bright sky,
Powered by the noisome, no-nonsense wind
Of March twenty-one.

To visit the new baby girl across the road,
She was to have shared my birthday,
But she chose St. Patrick's Day instead.

*Notes on Ireland and Other Writings*

I will listen to the wind-song of the cedar
trees
As it sends thrills of eerie delight down
my spine
The brook in the back lot will chuckle

And the "lull-lull-lull" of the Willapa
nearby
Murmuring forever,
Calling "Come. Come. Come."


8/15/78

*Notes on Ireland and Other Writings*

## December 7, 1941: A Study in Faith

Thunder of war-drums rolls around the
world.
Smoke of battle shrouds a sinister sky
Peace, shriveled and dead
The fragrance of the violets from springs
gone by.

Silent and sad, I seek the sanctuary
Of the poplar grove,
Motionless against the trees,
I breathe the chill fragrance of the coming
snow.

Twilight, and a wee wren murmurs
A sleepy greeting to the first lazy flakes
Falling, falling, softly, softly
The poplar's transposed now

Wee wren is silent now
Head tucked under wing,
Dreaming, dreaming, of the violet's
fragrance
In the coming spring.

2/25/77

*Notes on Ireland and Other Writings*

## The Murder

The spirit of the cedar tree
Dress softly green under the chiffon
Of her morning-mist veil.
Standing regal, queen of the forest.

She will die today.
The destroyers will come, with barbarous
weapons.
Saws with needle-teeth, and sharp axes
Unsheathed for murder.

A gentle shudder shakes her
dew-diamonds
To the forest floor.
The woodsmen are here now.
Awestruck, staring at the wonder of her.

No matter. She must go. And the thing is
done.
Falling, crying, dying,
She now lies on the forest floor.

*Notes on Ireland and Other Writings*

## Joy

Up, from winter dreams beneath the
mud,
Shimmering through spring sunlight,
honey-gold.
In perfect arcs they soar, alight on the lily
pads,
Dive with sportive glee into the pool.
Spring-warmed earth rejoices,
Greeting the Time of Life Returning.

*Notes on Ireland and Other Writings*

## Prisoner, Freed.

Endless eons gripped in my prison-rock,
I await my freeing.
My deliverer comes; my tight cage is
chopped, chiseled,
As shattered shards at my feet.
Perfect, I stand. Beautiful, free !!

Eons roll on. Civilization evolve, dissolve.
My creator, a handful of dust,
But I stand forever,
His gift to eternity,
Perfect, beautiful, free !!

# NANCY HENNESSY'S
# SHORT STORIES

# The Day of the Saint

Tassach stood on the Hill of Saul, in front of the first church in Ireland, which had once been the barn where the chieftain of the district kept his cattle. Until the day he met Tassach's master. Time was late afternoon. The date was the 17th of March, sometime in the latter half of the 5th Century.

There was definitely a chariot approaching the hill. Tassach peered through age-dimmed eyes, trying to see the occupant. Surely, surely, he knew that figure. Suddenly he started forward, hurrying down the path that led to the main road. Joy suffused his face as he came close to the chariot and helped the driver dismount.

"Patrick! How wonderful to see you. We did not expect you until summer! What brings you so early?"

Patrick, apostle to Ireland, showed the ravages of hard work and hardships and great age in his sun-tanned, lined old face; but, Tassach thought, nothing would ever dim the brilliance of those blue eyes. They sparkled with zest for life as he embraced

Tassach, his bishop, though he was now a very old man indeed.

After they had refreshed themselves the two old men settled down for a visit.

Patrick seemed filled with a secret joy. It fairly radiated from him. "Tassach," he said, "you asked why I came early to the Church of the Barn. As you know, I have always wanted to die and be buried here at Saul. I have come home to die. It will not be long now. My work is done and the time has come for me to hand it over to you and the others. The work of bringing the Faith to these Irish must continue. And Tassach, I am very, very tired. Bone-tired."

The old saint and his bishop talked until far into the night, planning for their church in Ireland. Suddenly Patrick dropped asleep and Tassach sat beside him, thinking of the glorious life of service and self-sacrifice of the man beside him. When a boy of 16 he had been captured by Irish sea-raiders and sold into slavery; in the end, though, it was he who had captured his captors and bound them with shackles of faith and love which they would never break.

Suddenly, Patrick woke. "It is now, Tassach. Now I must leave you." He kissed the cross which Tassach, weeping bitterly

*Notes on Ireland and Other Writings*

for the loss of a friend, held to his dying lips. He reached out and grasped Tassach's hand and pressed it.

And so they sat, the two old saints, until Tassach felt the hand he held in his relax and, looking, saw that Patrick had closed his eyes and rested.

## A Friend For Tommy

Tommy had no brothers or sisters. He and his parents lived in a tiny village named Frances, set like a shallow bowl amidst the Willapa Hills; the Willapa river flowed near his home and many streams flowed into it. The stream nearest to his house was Fern Creek, and it was toward Fern Creek that Tommy was trudging that hot, sleepy summer afternoon.

As he walked along he sang a song his grandmother had told him she sang when she was a little girl:

"Twenty froggies went to school, down beside a rushy pool, dum, dum, de dum. Twenty froggies grew up fast, bullfrogs they became at last. Now they sit on other logs, teaching other little frogs."

Tommy laughed suddenly. "I'll bet they had fun. And *they* were never lonesome." He had arrived at the creek. The water had backed up into the bank, making a wide, quiet pool with water lilies growing in the middle and a mossy log at the edge. Tommy sat on the log and stared for a long time into the pool. It certainly was a warm day. He yawned, then yawned again. He thought about how lonely he was. More

*Notes on Ireland and Other Writings*

than anything he needed a friend, now that he was five years old and allowed to go to the creek alone. He had been taught about the dangers of the creek. A friend would be a good thing to have. He yawned again, and his eyes closed.

"Ahem."

Tommy's eyes flew open. Beside him on the log sat a huge, green bullfrog.

"Excuse me," said the frog. "Do you mind if I sit here and relax a bit?" He sighed and mopped his brow with his hand. "Those upperclassmen get a bit out of hand as Commencement draws near. But the responsibility is making an old frog of me."

"That's too bad." Tommy was a very courteous little boy. "You are the first frog I ever met who could talk."

"Any frog can talk if you catch him at the right time of day," the frog replied.

"What time is it?" Tommy was also a curious little boy.

"Ah, that would be telling," said the frog with a mysterious look.

Tommy dropped the subject for a moment. "My name is Tommy. What's yours?"

The frog looked embarrassed. "Well," he said, "as a matter of fact, it's Floyd."

The frog's embarrassment was not lost on Tommy. "Don't you like it?"

"I can't stand it!" his new friend burst out bitterly. "It was given me when I was still a tadpole. I told them I'd rather have Figaro, but everybody just laughed and said, "Whoever heard of a frog named Figaro? Don't be silly. Floyd it is."

"Do you like being a school teacher, Floyd?"

"Well, yes, and then again no. The toddlers aren't so bad – and some of them are really cute. But as they get older they get into the smart-aleck stage. It was different when I was young, you can bet."

"If I come back tomorrow at exactly the same time, will you be able to talk to me?" Tommy found himself liking this wonderful new friend very much indeed.

"Probably not," answered Floyd. "The time changes from day to day and we never know until that morning what time it will be."

"Well, can I come tomorrow anyway? Maybe it will be the right hour."

"By all means do so," said Floyd cordially. "Be my guest. But now I must leave you. The hour is up."

He positioned himself for takeoff, and a moment later a perfect arc through the air, landing on a lily pad in the middle of the pool. He looked back to be sure that Tommy had seen and admired.

"Goodbye, Floyd," called Tommy. "I'll be waiting for you tomorrow afternoon."

Floyd waved a hand in friendly farewell. "G-r-r-k," he said, and was gone.

Tommy remained sitting on the log for a long time, thinking. Finally he stood up and started up the path toward home and supper.

"It just couldn't have been a dream that he talked to me," Tommy said to himself. "It was just too real. Anyway, I'll come every day to see Floyd, and it doesn't really matter if I come at the right hour or not. We're friends, and friends don't *have* to talk to understand each other. They just need to be *together*."

## The Tale of the Twins

The twins were sitting stiffly side by side in Judge Coleman's office. Rosemary glanced at Dierdre from under lowered lashes, but could detect no signs of the humiliation which flooded her own proud fifteen-year-old heart at the judge's words. But then, Dierdre's poker face would never let her down in a crisis. So much could not be said for Rosemary's, which mirrored every thought the moment it was born.

"You see, my dears," the judge was saying, "I'm afraid there is nothing left but the farm. When your father was alive he made a good income but of course he could not foresee that he would be cut down in the prime of life, or he would have made some provision for you. There isn't even insurance."

Judge Coleman was a kindly man, but in the present instance, somewhat embarrassed. Why did Hugh Richards have to leave him the guardianship of these two girls. He and his wife knew nothing about children. Not that these two were children, exactly. Fourteen or fifteen, he imagined. Dashedly attractive looking, too, or would be in a few years. The judge had always prided himself on possessing an eye for beauty. That flaming topknot would cause hearts to flutter, or he missed his guess. Yes, Miss Rosemary would set them raving all right.

It was Rosemary who spoke now. Her voice was extremely solemn. "Judge Coleman, what we want to know is, what is to be done about us. Of course Dierdre and I have talked about it a lot, and what we have decided is that we will have to find some way of earning our own living. Of course, I know we can't live out on the farm alone, so I suppose the best thing we can do for the present is to find some place to work for our room and board until we finish school. We'll be almost seventeen then, and practically grown up." Her words tumbled out excitedly, betraying her anxiety.

Dierdre gazed proudly and devotedly at her twin during this speech. She had no cnvy of her sister's ability to take the lead. She was a very feminine, second-the-motion sort of girl, and she was only too happy to have Rosemary shoulder the full responsibility in these frightening, unhappy days.

Much as he resented this duty that had been more or less thrust upon him, Judge

*Notes on Ireland and Other Writings*

Coleman could not restrain a twinkle of admiration. By George, these young ones had gumption, a trait made conspicuous by its absence in the young of today, in the judge's opinion.

"Well now, my dear young ladies," he began, "I'm sure that is a most worthy ambition. But do you realize just what it would mean, earning your way as you go. Having to give up parties and nice clothes and all the frills you ladies dote on." He watched Rosemary closely. Dierdre, for all intents and purposes, he had entirely forgotten.

It was Dierdre, however, who answered him.

"Of course we do," she replied. "We have come to the conclusion that there are certain things we will have to do. And certain other things we will have to wait to do, if our lives are to go the way we planned. For one thing, until we are through college, we are partners. If either of us succeeds in making any money we are going to put it into the common fund. We haven't thought of a way to earn any yet, but we will before long."

The judge listened in amazement to this precocious speech. It simply wasn't possible that these two contemplated facing the world on their own.

Well, why not, he thought. His own father had run away from home at fifteen, and had never gone back. Of course, he mused, girls were different. They had to have a certain amount of looking after in their own interests.

Even though his annoyance with Hugh Richards was fast diminishing in the presence of Hugh Richards' daughters, he still did not relish the task of shouldering the responsibility of their welfare. However a duty was a duty, and the kindly hearted judge would never forgive himself if they came to any harm as a result of his negligence.

Truth to tell, he was becoming more reconciled each moment to his fate. Darned fine looking girls they were, both of them, and he would jolly well encourage them in this idea of maintaining their self-respect.

\* \* \* \*

Rosemary and her sister had been staying with Mrs. Coleman and the judge since their father's funeral two days before.

That evening, after the return from the cemetery, the sisters had discussed their predicament, and arrived at their decision in the lovely Coleman garden facing Puget Sound.

They knew already of their destitute state. Destitute, that is, with the exception of a tumble-down ten acre farm about fifteen miles north of Seattle. It had been purchased by their father about a year before, with the intention of transforming it into a model farm. The idea had been inspired by a visit to Alderwood Manor and the chicken ranches in the vicinity. But two weeks later Hugh Richards had lost every cent he had in the world, and a year later he had died.

He died leaving his daughters to the care of Judge Coleman, the one among his friends who had protested against the business venture that ended so disastrously for him. It was the best he could do for them.

As usual, Rosemary was the first to speak of the subject that was uppermost in both their minds.

"I suppose we had better make up our minds just what we are going to do, Dee," she said slowly. "If we talk it over beforehand together and sort of decide on a course to follow and stick to it, no matter what anyone says, we may be able to accomplish something. If we don't, we're sunk. Just orphans, to be taken care of just as cheaply and quickly as possible."

"Not," she amended thoughtfully, staring out across the turquoise waters of the Sound, "that you can blame people for feeling that way. I suppose orphans are a nuisance if they haven't any money. But I think if we sort of beat them to the draw with a plan of our own, or make it seem like we have one, they won't be able to feel imposed upon. And it will rather take the wind out of their sails, which makes it that much more easy sailing for us."

Which was Rosemary all over. Carrying the war into the enemies territory was her idea of diplomacy. And to give her her due, she usually accomplished her object.

Dierdre agreed with these sentiments. Make it seem like they have a plan. As a matter of fact, she had been thinking practically the same thing herself. But as usual, she left it for Rosemary to give voice to the idea.

\* \* \* \*

Mrs. Coleman entered the judge's study with the full expectation of commiserating with him over the tight corner in which he found himself. She understood her husband thoroughly, and as a rule, could forecast his reactions unerringly. This, however, was not one of the times. True, the judge was pacing the floor, just as she had expected. But she had scarcely entered the door before she realized that he was considerably more perturbed than the occasion warranted, in her estimation.

She waited for the judge to giver her a cue, as usual. A quiet, gentle appearing little body she was. Her personality bore out the description, with a few notable exceptions. Despite her obvious mildness, she was capable of stating her mind most vigorously, without fear or favor. Even the judge, whom she considered the world's prize husband, was not exempt from the occasional 'curtain lecture'. But truth to tell, Marcella Coleman was not meek at all. She simply considered very few things worth getting into a bother over. When she did throw her hat into the ring, she was an ally to be valued and also an enemy to be feared.

The judge took a few more turns about the room, by way of clearing the air for conversation. Then, clearing his throat, he began tentatively.

"My dear, what on earth is to be done about these two youngsters? They are much too young to be thrown entirely on their own resources. Yet they have some outlandish notion of maintaining themselves. Of course the idea is preposterous. My conscience permit me to allow it, even if I didn't want to help them. And you know, Marcella, I have never said that I did not. All I said was, that the whole business was a nuisance and an imposition. And I still think that Hugh Richards would have been much more sensible if he had left his girls in the charge of someone who had raised several kids. Just the same, these are darned nice girls, and it seems a shame that they have no relatives to make a home for them."

He glanced at her desperately. The more he talked about it, the more urgently he wanted to convince her of his desire without actually putting it into words.

He need not have worried. Mrs. Coleman had not lived with the judge for thirty years for nothing. She refused to be stampeded, however, and took her time and chose her words carefully. She, too, had pondered much over the probable fate of the Richards' twins, in case the judge's brittle and crusty antagonism toward the young proved insurmountable an obstacle for his generous heart. Unlike the judge, though, she had come to a decision some time ago.

She scrutinized her spouse with a practiced eye. Now, she decided, was the moment to bring the judge to the decision which she had made for him some hours previously.

"Well, Henry, it isn't necessary for you to excite yourself about it. The matter simply boils down to this. Hugh Richards made you the legal guardian of his daughters without consulting your wishes in the matter. And I think that absolves you of any responsibility. You would be quite justified in refusing to have anything to do with it. No one would blame you for committing them to an orphanage until they are of age, if you did not want the inconvenience of a couple of girls running around. Though the girls themselves would not fare so well, I'm afraid."

She anticipated the judge's reaction so confidently that her voice fairly reeked with the complacency and satisfaction over a job well done.

He again cleared his throat, and half wondering just how much he was letting himself in for, replied.

*Notes on Ireland and Other Writings*

"Well, Marcella, considering everything, don't you think we could give it a trial? Perhaps they could do errands around the property or chores to help out. We have no money issues to really speak of, so perhaps an allowance would be warranted for them. That would help them earn their keep while here."

"Good heavens, Henry," she replied. "I shall enjoy myself tremendously. I have been getting old lately anyway. Too many bridge games and senile old women. But Henry, how long would you want this trial, and what of the plan when it ends?"

The judge thought for a moment. "These girls seem trapped between wanting to be girls and wanting to be independent. This age of course they are too young to be on their own. I believe Cousin Luke could be of assistance. He can help fix up the farm that was left them, and perhaps find them husbands in the future that can help them with the farm."

This suggestion surprised Marcella but she also liked it.

"Yes, Henry. They are too young now and would not know anything about the farm. But they can learn now and especially when older. Why don't you call Luke."

*Notes on Ireland and Other Writings*

\*   \*   \*   \*

The next morning, the twins took their places at the breakfast table, and were told of the plan.

"Now girls," started Marcella, "the judge and I have discussed this matter thoroughly, and it would be foolish indeed to not keep you here with us. You are now much too young to be capable of looking after yourselves properly. And to be quite frank about it, we shall enjoy having you about."

The judge looked at his wife and then the girls, and continued where she had left off. "We will allow you to stay here until you are done with school, with errands and chores for you which will earn you an allowance. Marcella's cousin is an old farm hand and he has agreed to help improve the farm that your father left. When you leave here, you can move to the farm. Since you have no relatives and no other place to go, that is the best we can do for you. Perhaps you can find husbands to help with the farm, or make a living on the farm, or even sell the farm if you wish."

Rosemary's eyes met her sisters. The judge and his wife were right, the twins were battling between being dependent and

132

independent. Now, if ever, was the moment to fight against dependence and all of its inherent evils. But she was cautious.

Dierdre, too realized the need for diplomacy. She feared that her sister would impulsively march in and do their cause irreparable harm. She chose to reply before her sister could speak.

"That is so wonderful of both of you," Dierdre began. "It would be wonderful to stay here. Like we said, we do want to try to help out, so errands and chores would be ok. The farm is very run-down and if it can be improved, then that would be great also. We can't thank you enough." After finishing, she shot a glance at Rosemary, who faintly nodded in return.

\* \* \* \*

Almost two years had gone by, and Mr. and Mrs. Coleman drove the girls to see their farm. Luke and some of his friends and co-workers had transformed the run-down place into quite the renovated farm. It was now not only ready to be lived in and on, but ready for crops.

Rosemary shot Dierdre a quick glance, not really knowing what to say or how to think. About two years of chores and errands and now this in front of them.

"So what do you think, girls?" Mr. Coleman asked. "When you leave our place, this farm is ready to go."

Lost in thought for a moment, Rosemary finally spoke up. "Oh yes, Mr. Coleman, Lester did a great job. Please thank him for us."

"It is Luke, not Lester," said Marcella.

"Oh, I'm sorry about that," said Rosemary.

Back at the Colemans' place, the girls went off to their bedroom. This was a bit much for them, to say the least. After talking among themselves for awhile, they came up with a plan of their own.

The next morning, Mrs. Coleman had pancakes and eggs ready for breakfast, as well as some of her delicious homemade cocoa. She and the judge sat down without the girls there. After a few minutes, Mrs. Coleman went to check on them.

Their bedroom door was closed, so she knocked. No answer. She opened the door, and gasped. Their belongings were gone and the window was open.

Rosemary and Dierdre were gone. Mrs. Coleman went to the kitchen to tell the judge, and broke into tears.

*Notes on Ireland and Other Writings*

\*   \*   \*   \*

So in the end, what of the tale of the twins? What was their cause?

It is simple. People were there who cared for them and tried to help them and offered a way for them. Like many youth of today, they were ungrateful and wanted freedom without responsibility.

## A Depression Memory

Mary Martin stood at the foot of the rickety staircase which led to the apartment where blind old Angus MacDougal lived with his blind collie dog. She could feel it in her bones; this case was going to be different. A caseworker could always tell, when the spine began to tingle and tension mounted by the minute. She mounted the worn stairs and knocked on the door of Apartment 5.

She had often seen old Angus and his dog walking down Hastings Street towards Main in the rain, an ancient green window blind draped over the dog's back in lieu of a raincoat. Now the organization she worked for had given her the old man's name with instructions to induce him to give up his news stand, get rid of his dog, and go to a home for the blind.

At last the door opened and Angus stood peering out. He was holding a partially knitted sock in his hand. Mary noted that he knew how to turn a neat heel. The old collie stood beside him, and the delicious fragrance of beef stew was also in the air.

*Notes on Ireland and Other Writings*

She said, "Good evening, Angus. My name is Mary Martin, and I would like to come in and visit you for awhile. May I?"

"Come in, ma'am. You are very welcome." She could sense the thoughts he was having behind those blind eyes of his...another do-gooder, she means well, but why don't they just leave me alone....

She looked curiously about the tiny apartment. It was immaculate. Waves of heat from a wood-burning stove had driven out the November chill, and it was very warm. So far, so good. The stew was simmering on an oil range, and the table was set for supper. As she took the chair old Angus offered, she studied the contents of that table. A sliced tomato, half a loaf of rye bread, a two-inch wedge of cheese. In the center a geranium plant in a tomato can flaunted one brave red blossom defiantly above the red-checked tablecloth. A large cake, obviously bought in the market, bore the words "Happy anniversary, Angus and Eben."

"Is it a birthday?" she asked.

"No, ma'am. It's the anniversary of the day Eben here came to me, in a time of great trouble. After my wife died, life just didn't seem worth living. It got so bad I decided to end it and planned to jump from one of

*Notes on Ireland and Other Writings*

the high buildings. But before I could, one November evening I opened the door and the rain and wind came tearing into our little house, and in crept this shivering, half-starved little pup. I couldn't go off and leave him, so I dried him off and put him by the stove to get warm while I fixed him warm bread and milk. We've been together ever since. I reckon we always will be."

He paused for a moment and then said suddenly, "Eben and me, we'd be right pleased, ma'am, if you would stay and share our dinner."

On sudden impulse she accepted, though she had not intended to. But she liked this courageous old man and his dedicated old dog. Angus picked up Eben's dish, filled it with the bubbling stew and set it aside to cool.

"How did you happen to name him Eben?" she asked.

"I named him for a dog I had when I was a lad back in Scotland. Ah, he was a fine dog too." He cut a large slice of cake and held it out for the dog. Eben wolfed it down and licked his lips, grinning his thanks.

Mary braced herself. This wasn't going to be easy. She said gently, "Angus, we heard about your dog becoming blind. Life can be very hard for an animal that has lost his sight. And you, yourself – wouldn't it be easier if you lived in a nice home with other elderly people to talk to? Don't you feel that it is time to give up your news stand and retire? I know a lovely place you could go."

Angus sensed the gentle trap. "And could Eben come too?" he asked keenly.

Mary bit her lip, feeling sudden shame. "Well, no, Angus. You see, there is no provision made there for dogs. But we would take care of Eben for you. Euthanasia is a merciful death. You need not worry at all. He would not suffer."

The more she said, the worse she felt.

She managed to continue. "Angus, Eben is very old. And he is blind. Don't you believe it would be better that way?"

"No, ma'am. I don't." The reedy old voice suddenly swelled with unexpected strength. "After my wife Margaret died, I wanted to dic too. So much I planned to take my own life, God forgive me. When Eben came, and looked at me with those big brown eyes of his, I knew he had been sent to help me. He's a fine dog, Eben is. In his prime, we did everything, and went everywhere, together. Life became a fine thing again."

He paused before continuing. "Then my sight began to go. It was pretty bad, all right. But I had Eben. Without him, I don't know what would have become of me. He guided me everywhere. He was awfully smart, as smart as most people. Then, maybe a year or so ago, he began to change, as if he wasn't sure anymore. As if he had to feel his way like I did. I took him to a vet and was told that he was going blind and nothing could be done to help him."

Turning directly towards Mary, he continued, "Ma'am...your offer is kindly meant, I'm sure. But Eben and me, we'll be shipmates until one of us has to start down that long road alone. I pray every day that Eben will be the first to go, and even though I will miss him terribly, I could muddle through somehow. It would be different for Eben. He wouldn't know what to do. It worries me sure, ma'am."

Mary left shortly after that. She could not get the old man out of her mind. Why did this old man and his dog worry her? She had a restless night and dawn found her hollow-eyed with fatigue, but she had reached a decision. Later she went out into the stormy November morning. Once on Hastings she could see old Angus and

*Notes on Ireland and Other Writings*

Eben half a block ahead, slowly making their way to the tiny news stand. Eben wore his usual window-blind raincoat. They reached the news stand and Angus drew out his rickety camp stool and sat down.

Mary quickened her steps now. She would tell Angus her decision to give Eben a home with her if he was left alone. Suddenly she stopped. Angus laid his hand on Eben's aged head, and the old dog laid his muzzle on his knee and raised his dimming eyes towards his master's face. Mary felt the sudden sting of tears coming in her eyes, and a bystander turned to stare at her as she exclaimed, "How beautiful! Oh, how beautiful they are!"

*Notes on Ireland and Other Writings*

## The Cat That Walked Alone

Miss O'Toole paused at the window of her warm, comfortable living room and glanced out at the storm. The sleet on the roof and the wind howling down the chimney made a half pleasant, half mournful sound. Miss O'Toole shivered in sympathy for those who were forced to go out on an evening like this. Then she faced her guest, who was on the verge of departure.

"I'm real sorry, Mrs. Donovan, that you can't stay longer. But the weather seems to be getting worse and worse all the time. It's terribly cold for St. Patrick's Day, isn't it? Well, I'll be over in a few days if the rain ever lets up. Good-bye."

Before Miss O'Toole closed the door on her departing guest, she noticed an old cat walking alone along the driveway past her house. She called out to the cat, but no reply, not even a glance her way. After watching the cat out in the storm for another minute or so, she closed the door.

She walked into her snug little dining room. Laying out her dinner dishes she thought, "I've been living here alone in this house since I was twenty-five years old. Ever since my father died, thirty years

142

ago. I like my own company, too. But it is nice to have someone drop in for a word now and then. One does get lonesome.... now where in the name of common sense did I put those crackers?"

Meanwhile, the old cat continued. His goal was the garbage can at the end of the street that he had discovered the day before. Why he did not have a warm house to go to and why he shunned humans was not known.

There had been some burnt oatmeal beside the garbage can and now the cat was making his way to it in the forlorn hope that there would be something there he could eat. Not that he was fond of eating out of garbage cans, you understand. But a stomach that has been empty for twenty-four hours loses much of its fastidiousness.

He reached the garbage can and looked around, and even peered in and sniffed. No luck. Discouraged, he turned around and headed the other way, gaunt and old, and gray as an old man.

Miss O'Toole was looking out the window at the storm when the old cat went past. Again, the cat did not look her way or even look up, continuing with his head down and walking alone.

*Notes on Ireland and Other Writings*

## Friends and Helpers

Lately my mind often travels back – way back to my early childhood, and my friends among those women and girls who came to help my mother take care of me. Mother would much rather do housework and cook than entertain an obstreperous child with a bump of curiosity which she found appalling. So, during the first years of my life, came Mrs. Smith and her daughter Mamie, Mary Ashton, Christy, Ethel, Mrs. Jewell, and Mrs. Finley, whose little boy Clyde was just my age and came with his mother when she worked for us.

Mrs. Smith was the first. She was a practical nurse and very superstitious. She was there when I was born and during my infancy. I was a very sickly baby and I almost didn't make it, so my parents wanted a person who had a lot of experience. The first time my mother started to trim my fingernails after I was born, Mrs. Smith was horrified. She took me in her lap and proceeded to chew those fingernails down. Then my mother was horrified and demanded an explanation. Mrs. Smith told her, "Now you'll never need to worry that she will grow up to be a thief. This will insure her honesty."

Mrs. Smith had five children, besides two who died in infancy. Her husband had escaped from the city jail where he was being held for trial on a charge of statutory rape. She told my mother, "I hope they never catch him. As long as he is on the run, he'll never dare come back here. I hope I never have to see him again." Mother told me years later that he had lived off her earnings ever since she married him.

When I was one and a half years old, her daughter Mamie was just starting high school. She was looking for a part-time job to pay her way. She was a lovely girl and my parents hired her to come in the morning and get me up and dressed and get the breakfast; then to come back after school and stay until the supper dishes were done. The going wage for this type of job was $1.50 per week, but my folks liked Mamie so much that they increased it to $2.00 per week.

I loved Mamie. She occasionally covered for me when I had misbehaved. I very much liked to get my mother's high dress shoes, lace them tightly to the top, then knot them over and over until they were almost impossible. When I did this, I invariably

145

had the unlovely task of unknotting and unlacing them myself. But the last time my mother had promised me a spanking if I did it again; instead Mamie found the shoes, laced and knotted, before my mother did, and I can remember vividly the picture of her hurriedly undoing my misdeed. That was one spanking I escaped. I wasn't usually that lucky.

Mamie was beautiful, tall, with dark eyes and beautiful dark hair. When her graduation approached, my mother gave Mrs. Smith the suit she had bought for her honeymoon to make an outfit for Mamie. It was gray, but Mrs. Smith dyed it crimson and made her a beautiful outfit. She came over to show us how it looked on that Sunday morning and she was dazzlingly beautiful. The crimson was just right for her coloring.

We moved to Frances right after that and I never saw Mamie again. Mrs. Smith died a few months after we moved, and Mamie went down to Hollywood to try to break into the movies. She was one of the lucky ones and made a hit right away. She made some pictures with Frances X. Bushman and then married him. Her screen name was Beverly Bayne. After their son, Frances X. Bushman Jr., was born, Mamie retired

*Notes on Ireland and Other Writings*

from the movies to take care of him. Mamie was always crazy about little kids. I hope she had a happy life; she deserved it.


(-to be continued-)


Bellingham, Washington
June 1978

(Editor's note: nothing about the other people has been found in my aunt's papers or notes.....)

# The Widow Machree, Macushla, and St. Patrick

Once long ago, in Ireland, there lived a poor widow, whom everyone called Widow Machree. Her first name was Moira, but only her husband had called her that, so now it was almost forgotten by her neighbors. She was so poor that the only food she had were the eggs laid by her two faithful hens, the potatoes and other vegetables she raised in her tiny garden patch, and the milk from her beautiful white cow Macushla. There was a monastery nearby, and the monks, pitying her sad plight, often brought her honey. The widow repaid the kindness with the rich cream from Macushla's milk.

Life had not always been so bitterly hard. Sean, her husband, with the wild red hair coming to a peak on his forehead, was a fisherman. He was successful in a modest way and they raised a garden on their little patch of ground, and had made their house snug and secure against the winter storms. And they had bought the beautiful white heifer Macushla, who was the pride and delight of their lives. She grazed with the neighbor cows on the common grazing land, but she was so tame that she would follow them about like a faithful dog.

One morning Sean stood in the open doorway looking out to sea. He turned back, picked up his old clay pipe from the mantle and lighted it. Then he sat down, straddling one of their two kitchen chairs.

Sean's movements were always slow and deliberate. He puffed on his pipe for a few moments, then said, "I doubt it will blow up a storm today, Moira. I think I'll take the boat out."

Moira waved good-bye from the shore. Tonight he would return, with his boat full of fish. But that afternoon a terrible storm blew, and Sean never returned. Moira then became known as the Widow Machree.

Four years passed. Macushla waxed sleek and beautiful, so beautiful that she was the wonder of the countryside. The widow brushed and curried her every day; and when the long warm summers were over and the howling winds from the north Atlantic swept over Ireland, Macushla was warm and happy in her little shelter.

One especially cold night the widow went to milk the cow, carrying as usual a pail of hot water. She placed the milking stool beside Macushla and the pail of water beside it. She dipped her ice-cold hands into the hot water and held them there until they were warm. Macushla must not be startled by the touch of her cold fingers.

She looked up at the cow. "Macushla," she began, "that thieving, plundering chief MacCuill saw you today and tried to buy you. As though I would ever part with you. Least of all to the likes of him."

The powerful chief MacCuill was a greedy and violent man indeed. Much of his wealth was booty brought back from his plundering expeditions, as well as the robbery of poor people who were unable to protect themselves. His eyes had blazed with rage at the widow's curt refusal to part with her cow Macushla. She was afraid he might have her murdered and simply take Macushla. Such deeds were common for MacCuill, as she well knew.

Macushla turned her gentle, dark eyes trustfully towards her. The widow vowed to herself that, come what may, MacCuill should never have her. But how to prevent it? A powerful friend might help. The monks at the monastery were the most powerful people in the district. Their influence was tremendous.

The next morning she lost no time getting to the monastery, though she arrived in a sorry state. She had slipped and fallen headlong on a patch of red clay which last night's rain had washed down from the high clay bank along the road.

She explained to the prior and he looked very troubled. "In truth, my dear widow, you might be wise to let him have the cow. She is a prize animal, the most beautiful I have ever seen. That is why this evil man wants her."

"Never," she retorted. "I may be forced to flee from the district and take Macushla with me, but MacCuill shall never lay his hands on her."

The prior was thoughtful. "The great Patrick is visiting here at the monastery just now. He is here for the express purpose of dealing with that ruffian MacCuill. I fear that Patrick will be disappointed. MacCuill is beyond reaching. But we will go to Patrick's quarters and see what he thinks should be done. I hope he can help you."

The Widow Machree knew all about the great Patrick, but she had never seen him. She looked at him curiously and liked what she saw. A tall man with a stubborn chin and steadfast eyes. Yes, he would help her.

On hearing her story Patrick smiled grimly. "He doesn't know it yet, but MacCuill and I have an appointment with

*Notes on Ireland and Other Writings*

destiny very soon. But come, we will go and view this marvelous cow, and decide what is to be done."

When St. Patrick saw Macushla, his eyes widened in appreciation of her perfection. The widow's heart swelled with pride at this tribute from the saint. "Widow," he said, "let us see if we can outsmart the great MacCuill. The first thing to do is to get some of that red clay I saw as I was coming down the road."

Patrick picked up a handful of the wet clay and smeared it on Macushla's nose. The widow gasped and Macushla herself backed away, startled. Patrick only said, "Steady, girl. This isn't going to hurt you."

He proceeded to plaster the red clay over every inch of her body, turning her into a rough-coated, rusty red nondescript creature. Patrick surveyed her and was well pleased with his efforts.

Poor Macushla. She did not understand, but it was her nature to trust. And trust she did, rubbing her nose forgivingly against Patrick's hand.

"Now," Patrick said, "she is ready to graze with the other cows."

A short time later when MacCuill went to the common grazing land to look at Macushla, he saw no sign of the beautiful white animal. He never cast a glance at the pitiful-looking reddish creature hanging her head as though ashamed of her appearance.

He hurried to the widow's house. "Where is Macushla?" He demanded. "If you have sold her to anyone else I'll have your heart's blood. I swear it."

The widow was terribly frightened, but stood her ground. "You'll never find her. She is well hidden, and a long way from here."

MacCuill tried another tactic. "Tell me where she is," he coaxed, "and I will make you rich. I must have that cow. She is the most beautiful in all of Ireland."

Just then Patrick arrived at the widow's house. "I thought I would find you here, MacCuill," he said sharply. "Come with me. I want a few words with you."

The widow stared dumbfounded as the man who was the terror of the countryside sheepishly followed the saint out the door and up the road towards the monastery.

She did not see either of them for several days. Then one morning they appeared side by side on her doorstep. Patrick's face wore an expression of triumph, and she could hardly believe the change in

MacCuill. The erstwhile bully now wore an expression of sadness and shame.

"MacCuill has something to say to you," Patrick announced without preamble.

MacCuill lifted his head and she saw nothing but good-will in his eyes. "I will never persecute any man or woman ever again. Patrick has helped me to become a new man. Have no fear for Macushla now. She is perfectly safe. I am going on a voyage far away from here. I wish you every happiness all of the days of your life."

With that, he turned away and walked slowly up the road.

"Widow," said St. Patrick, "let us first restore Macushla to her former beauty, and then I have a favor to ask." As they cleaned the clay from an appreciative Macushla's coat he explained.

"When I was on the south coast a few years ago, they brought me a poor fellow who was unable to remember who he was or where he belonged. He had been found wandering on the beach. I have had him with me ever since. But I am forced to make many journeys, and these seem to make his trouble worse. Each new place he tries to remember if it is his home, and when he can't remember he broods about it. So I believe he should be settled in a perma-

*Notes on Ireland and Other Writings*

nent home. I would like to put him in that little place near the grazing common, but there should be someone there to clean his house and cook his food. He would never remember to do it himself. Would you do it?"

The widow's kind heart filled with pity for the poor man. And it would be a good way to repay Patrick. She agreed readily.

She went to the monastery with Patrick to meet the man. When one of the monks brought him into the room, she almost collapsed. A tall man, with wild red hair coming to a peak on his forehead.

"Sean?" she asked faintly. "Sean?"

The vague, hazy gaze wavered and finally settled on her, and his eyes met hers. "Moira," he faltered, as memory came flooding back. "Moira, it really is you. No dream. I've dreamed it so often, only I couldn't see your face."

Moira was almost in tears, but she made a great effort to not give way to emotions before the monks.

"Come home now, Sean. I can hardly wait for you to see Macushla. She has grown more beautiful than ever. She'll be wanting to see you, too."

155

## Macushla's New Friend

It was a week after the big rain when the Shannon overflowed its banks. The countryside was turned into a devastated horror. As the people slowly straggled back from the hills where they had taken refuge, they stared in disbelief at the unbelievable piles of debris covering their neat little gardens. Mud was everywhere – the flowers were covered with it. Even the weeds were choked in mud. Time to start cleaning up. They started immediately.

The first thing to do was to scrape the six-inch deep mud carpet from the common land where the community grazed their cattle. No Irish cow could be expected to stand all day in six inches of mud. When the mud was finally scraped away, they poured tons of water on the land to wash the grass so it would be clean and edible. At last, the land was ready for the cows.

Sean and several of the other men of the village went back up the hill to bring down the cows. The cows were patiently awaiting their return to the home pasture. Macushla was worth a hundred cows for her calming influence on the other cows, who were understandably nervous and

*Notes on Ireland and Other Writings*

skittery. She field-marshaled the herd down the hill and sedately moved forward onto the washed clean grazing land. The people stared, fascinated. Never has there been a cow such as Macushla. Without assistance from Sean and the others, she had taken command of her own kind and led them safely home.

And now the people of the other villages nearby came to claim their own cattle, for all the cows in the territory had been taken to the hill for safety. The cows were all sorted out and every cow but one was claimed. She was an elderly, gaunt, obviously ill-fed cow. The other cows, with the exception of Macushla, looked at her askance. But Macushla nudged her nose in a friendly way and had obviously taken a fancy to the famished-looking stranger cow.

No one claimed her. Some wanted to kill her as a useless thing eating the food of working animals. Her working days were long past. But Sean said, "Macushla doesn't think she is worthless. Look how friendly she is to the poor creature. I feel Macushla has earned the right to keep this animal. At least, we may find out where she came from."

And so it was decided. The poor old cow became Macushla's property for the time being, and grazed on the common with the other cows, and waxed fat and handsome. Her dingy coat took on a real luster. They called her Nasturtium.

One day a man came from a nearby village, and when he saw Nasturtium he gasped in surprise. "That is most certainly Barney Muldoon's cow that he turned out to starve when she got too old to give milk. His neighbors nearly drove him out of the village for his uncivilized behavior. A real mean one is Barney Muldoon."

At last they knew. Sean felt that under such circumstances, there was no need to let this Muldoon character know that his cow was here in the village. So time passed, and the friendship between Macushla and Nasturtium was beautiful to see.

Then one day it happened. A huge, brutal-looking hulk of a man came to the village. The first thing he spotted was Nasturtium standing beside her dear friend Macushla. He knew her immediately. But this cow was sleek and healthy looking. No matter. She was his cow, and he meant to have her back. He seized Nasturtium by the collar and attempted to drag her away. Nasturtium recognized him too, and she

*Notes on Ireland and Other Writings*

pulled back in horror. Macushla, seeing this, gave the man a painful poke on the arm with her horn. Just then Sean and some of the villagers came up to see what the disturbance was about. The stranger was holding his arm, and Macushla – yes, dear and mild Macushla – stood legs braced, fire in her eyes, ready to do battle.

"That's my cow," the man snarled. "I'm Barney Muldoon, and this – this – animal won't let me take her."

As far as the villagers were concerned, that settled it. Macushla was in the right. She always was. Sean said mildly, "Well, we will have the Brehon decide the matter, once and for all."

So off to the Brehon they all went, Sean leading Macushla and Nasturtium bringing up the rear.

When they reached the Brehon, he looked in surprise at the two cows. "What's all this?" he asked. He was a just man, but he was also one of Macushla's most ardent admirers.

Barney Muldoon said gruffly, "This miserable animal belongs to me. This other cow attacked me and refuses to let me take her. I want justice."

The Brehon looked him over, not liking what he saw. "I understand that you

*Notes on Ireland and Other Writings*

turned Nasturtium out to starve when you thought she was past her usefulness. How about that?"

"That is neither here nor there," was the man's retort. "That cow is mine. I want her. It's as simple as that."

"Not quite," the Brehon replied. "There is the matter of the animal's board and lodging to settle before you take possession." He turned away and consulted Sean and the others in a voice so low that the irate Muldoon could not hear. Then he turned back. "We have decided to charge you one thousand screpalls a day for board and lodging. After that the law says you may take the animal, God pity her."

"One thousand screpalls!" shrieked Muldoon. "It's robbery. She isn't worth it. I won't pay it. Keep the blasted cow."

He turned and strode towards the door. As he passed Nasturtium, he turned and kicked her savagely on the flank. And Nasturtium? Well, as far as he was concerned, Nasturtium had had it! As he passed, she lifted her hind hoof and in return she planted a beautiful, satisfying kick right on the right spot. Then she resumed her usual mild demeanor. Muldoon howled and shot through the door.

160

*Notes on Ireland and Other Writings*

The others applauded their appreciation, Macushla mooed congratulations, and Nasturtium modestly cast down her eyes and blushed until she was now red – all over.

Bellingham, Washington
July 1978

## Liverlip Goes to the Christmas Program

By Jo Reseigh, for Nancy Hennessy

Liverlip is a shaggy gray donkey that lives with Billy and his folks on a ranch in western Colorado. The high mountains full of oil shale shelter the ranch.

It is the Christmas season. The program at the one-room school is to be this evening.

Billy yells at his mother, "Hurry, Mom. Dad is coming with the sled."

It had snowed just enough so they could go in the sled which Daddy used to take feed to the cattle in the winter. The big black horses that were pulling the sled had tinkling bells fastened to their harnesses. Billy knew this was the only way to go in the winter, the cars were for summer. The big black horses, Dobbin and Robbin, were moving their big black hooves in rhythm to the bells. They knew this was a special night. Billy thought how beautiful they looked against the white snow as their black coats shone.

Mom came out of the house, wearing red stocking cap and mittens, and carrying a container with treats for the party after the program.

Billy was so excited he couldn't stand still. There were only 16 children in the school, so each one had to work hard to put on a program. He was a king in the play, and also a king in the pageant. Mom had said, "Good. Only one costume to make."

Soon they were all tucked in the sled, the goodies in a safe place, and a large warm blanket over their knees.

"Goodbye, Liverlip, we won't be too long."

Liverlip waved his large ears back and forth and watched them go, and then lay down.

Mother, Daddy and Billy sang carols as they went down the road. Several cars passed them, but Billy didn't care. Riding in a sled was more fun. When they reached the school the yard was filling up with cars, and also two other sleds. Daddy found a good place for the horses before they went into the school.

Inside there was a lot of noise and confusion, and also happiness. The small school was decorated with pine bows and red ribbons. At the back was the small tree that the children had decorated at school that day. There was also a table with a bright

*Notes on Ireland and Other Writings*

red cloth almost covered with goodies. The room was hot so a back window had been opened.

Everyone became quiet when the teacher stood in front of the room. The program went as the teacher had hoped it would. They were singing the song "Silent Night" when all of a sudden a very loud noise came in through the window – HEW HAW HE HAW......

Liverlip had decided he wanted to see the program too. After the people got over being startled they laughed and said, "Liverlip wanted to come too." Billy gave him a candy cane and told him to go home, but Liverlip stayed and waited to follow his folks home.

*Notes on Ireland and Other Writings*

# I Wanted The Moon

(Editor's note: This story by my aunt is very similar to my aunt's story called "The Moon and Ellen Adele" which was previously published in the book "Spoken In Due Season" in 1979 from the Writing Class at the Senior Activity Center in Bellingham, Washington. That story is included as the last of my aunt's short stories.)

\* \* \* \*

When I was about 3 years old I had a wild love affair with the moon. I would place my hands flat on the window pane and gaze, murmuring endearments all the while.

Finally I decided that it would be a nice thing to hold it in my arms. No amount of explanation would convince me that this was an impossibility.

One August night after I had gone to bed, I rose quietly and stood at the window in my usual worshipping stance, singing softly to it under my breath. The maple tree on the lawn cast its long shadow on the front porch.

I could stand it no longer. I put on my bedroom slippers and went very quietly out of the house, carefully keeping in the shadow of the huge maple tree.

Once on the dusty road all I had to do was keep walking eastward towards the moon, which stood just above the cedar grove on the hill. I wondered fleetingly how I would get it down once I reached it. That thought was put aside for the moment. I'll worry about that when I get there.

I kept getting pebbles in the slippers and they began to hurt. I sat down and took them off, placing them neatly side by side at the edge of the road. Then I walked on, the dust sifting through my toes, and I could feel it caking on my feet. The hill seemed farther away with each step. I was beginning to feel very tired, and hungry.

At last I saw a light far ahead. I walked on and saw that it was a small campfire at the edge of the grove. Two men sat there, and they were eating. One had a long gray beard and looked very kind and a little sad. I was not afraid of them.

I walked over to the campfire. The two men stared at me but did not speak.

I said, "I knew who you were right away because of your beard. You're God, aren't you?"

They continued to stare for a moment. Then the bearded one cleared his throat.

"Look here, little girl, it is way too late for you to be out. Go back home."

I replied, "I am looking for the moon. I want the moon. Can you help me get it?"

"Little girl," he said with some sadness in his voice, "I have been following that moon my entire life. I've had no luck. Give it up, little girl, and go home. That moon up there is a snare and a delusion."

I looked at him for a moment, then looked down at the food. "What is that?" I asked.

"That's beans. We have some left so I will dish you up some." The bearded man put some beans in a dish and also gave me a hot dog. After I polished off the beans and hot dog I felt much better. This was my first experience with a hot dog and boy was it delicious.

Then the subject returned to the matter at hand. "God," I said, still thinking the bearded man was God, "I still want to get to the moon. It is so close now, I'm sure I can."

The man tells her that the moon will shine light on the night sky, but cannot leave its ordained place in the heavens.

*Notes on Ireland and Other Writings*

"I'm sleepy," I said after yawning. The men continued at the campfire, but I leaned back against one of the nearby trees and slept. I awoke much later to the sound of a man's voice.

"There she is, asleep!" Half awake, I realized it was my father. He ran over to me, wrapped an ancient gunny sack around me and held me.

"What was it, dear? Why did you run away like that? If we hadn't found your slippers we would have no idea where to look for you."

I looked over at the burned out campfire. The two men were gone.

"Oh I was all right, Daddy," I said. "God and his friend were here and they looked after me. I came to get the moon but God said that it has to stay in its own place. Why did God go away, Daddy?"

"I don't know, dear. But God has an awful lot of little girls that he has to look after. Perhaps that is why he had to go."

As I look back, that happened seventy years ago last month. In the years since I have pondered the riddle of the man I called God. He obviously was an educated man, a kindly man, and a man whose spirit radiated goodness. Why did that happen? I will probably never know. It is one of the

*Notes on Ireland and Other Writings*

mysteries of life. But someday, I hope to find out.

## The Cedar Tree

When I was very small I spent much time at my grandfather's homestead, which was pure paradise to a little girl.

Near the boundary fence stood a large fir tree, just right for a swing, and Grandpa lost no time providing one for me. I was afraid to swing very high, but would sit gently swaying, deep in meditation.

On the other side of the boundary fence lived Mr. Crowley, crusty and cross. But in his yard, close to the fence, stood two beautiful cedar trees, symmetrical and serene in their perfection.

I had no other children to play with, but I was never lonely. The nearby world was much too fascinating.

One morning I was sitting in my swing and wished I had the courage to really pump up the motion. Suddenly I heard a voice saying, "It would be a lot more fun if you would stand up in the swing and start pumping. It would be like flying."

I looked around, but no one was there. Then the voice spoke again. "Here I am, over here, on the other side of the fence."

Sure as can be, the cedar tree was talking!

"I'm afraid to go high," I confessed, also rather ashamed.

"I know you are," the tree responded. "But do it a little at a time and you'll be used to it before you know it."

I tried it, and while I was very shaky at first I was soon soaring through the air, imagining myself as a bird flying. It was glorious!

The next day the tree said to me, "By the way, this is my little sister. She is very shy and doesn't talk much to people, but she likes you."

"How do you do," I said in my best manner. The smaller tree rustled her branches, but said nothing. But how pretty she was!

After that I talked to the cedar trees every day. I found out many things about the world from the talkative tree. One day I asked, "if you couldn't be a cedar tree, would you be a fir, like my swing tree?"

"What a question!" The tree was indignant. "I couldn't even imagine being anything but a cedar tree. Only people try to be what they are not. Take St. Patrick's Day, for instance. Every Frenchman, German, Swede and what-have-you dons a green garment and calls himself an Irishman. Silly, and I have no use for it.

Not that there's anything wrong with being an Irishman. It's just fine, if you *are* an Irishman."

That was a wonderful summer. In August Grandpa took me to the circus. I could hardly wait to get home to tell it all to my friend the cedar tree....the lions, the tigers, the elephants, the clowns.... everything!

Mr. Crowley and his hired hands were in his yard by the cedar trees. But wait, there was only *one* tree there now. Even as I stood, staring, the saws were working and then, with a great rending cry my cedar tree friend plunged to the earth and died.

Mr. Crowley came to the fence, saying to Grandpa, "I finally got rid of those trees. Now I'll have room to plant a monkey-puzzle tree there."

As I turned away, Grandpa tried to comfort me. "It's okay, dear. Mr. Crowley could not possibly understand. You see, the cedar tree never spoke to him. And he couldn't hear them if they did."

People still exclaim over and admire that monkey-puzzle tree as it stands there in the place of my cedar tree friend. What do I think? Ugly, grotesque, and out of place.

## Mary

This is the story about a little girl named Mary. Mary had a Daddy, and a Mommy, and two great big brothers, whose names were Alan and Mike. Alan and Mike were very good to her and played with her often. Mary liked them very much. She also had a dog whose name was Debbie, a cat named Susie and a cat named Pete. Susie and Pete purred when Mary petted them. Debbie could not purr, but smiled when Mary patted her head.

They had always lived in a yellow house but one day Mary's daddy began loading the tables and chairs on a trailer. When Mary asked him why he did that he said, "This is the day we move into the new house. We are going to live there now."

After some of the beds had been moved to the new house her daddy and mommy, with Alan and Mike, went with Mary in the car to the new house.

One day after Mary moved into the new house, she woke up to see the sun shining in the window. Today for her breakfast she had milk, toast, and prunes. She liked the milk and the toast but most of all she liked the prunes. After breakfast Mommy said,

*Notes on Ireland and Other Writings*

"Mary, let us go out into the yard and pick some more prunes, for you have eaten all we have for breakfast."

So they took a big basket and went out to the prune tree. There were lots of prunes on the tree, which her mommy picked and put into the basket. Some had dropped off the tree onto the ground, and those Mary picked up and put into the basket. The prunes on the tree were too high for her to reach. These were red prunes and were very good.

There was another tree beside the prune tree which had big juicy red apples hanging on its branches, and also on the ground below where they had fallen. Mary picked out the very nicest and prettiest one and put it in the basket with the prunes. There was a fence around the yard and growing beside the fence were many vines and flowers. There was a vine with big green leaves which Mommy said was ivy, and a grape vine with big bunches of juicy purple grapes. Mary's mommy picked a bunch of the grapes and lay them beside the big red apple in the basket of prunes. She then picked a big bunch of the vine with the green leaves.

Then Mary called, "Come, Pete. Come, Susie."

*Notes on Ireland and Other Writings*

Mommy followed Mary by saying, "Let us all go into the house, and I will let you help me make something pretty for the table to surprise Daddy when he comes home tonight."

So they went in and Mommy took a pretty basket out of the cupboard. Then she took the bunch of purple grapes, the big red apple, one of the prunes, and one of the green ivy vines, and put them into the basket so that they looked pretty.

That night when Daddy came home he looked at the pretty basket on the table and said, "My, my! That looks just too good to eat. But let's try this apple, and see how it tastes."

He bit into the great juicy red apple and said, "Umm. Perfect. I wonder if the prune is as good as the apple. Mary, will you try the prune and tell me if it is really good?"

Mary didn't need to be told twice to try the prune, and in no time at all it was gone and she said, "Daddy, that is the nicest prune I ever ate."

But then she saw that the apple and prune were gone, and she said sadly, "Oh, look. We've spoiled the basket. It isn't pretty anymore."

As the day was ending, so also is the story about little Mary.

*Notes on Ireland and Other Writings*

Mommy said, "Don't worry. Tomorrow we will fill the basket with flowers from our new garden, and it will be pretty again!"

*Notes on Ireland and Other Writings*

## Nursing Home Christmas

When my mother went to a nursing home three years before her death, I decided to spend every other day with her as she was blind and bedridden. She liked to have me report all the news, then read mystery stories to her – she was a great mystery buff. But she spent most of the day sleeping which left me free to circulate among the other patients. Many of these were retarded in varying degrees, from three-year-old mentalities to a simple inability to remember what day it was. I found these people to be both pathetic and appealing. There was something very sweet about them, the way a good child is sweet – sweet and trusting. I grew very attached to them, and learned much about their backgrounds.

As the Christmas season approached, I began to realize just how alone many of these people were. Relatives lived far away, or were dead, or were not interested. I began to think of ways to add a little Christmas cheer to the lives of these forlorn ones.

I knew it wasn't going to be easy, for these people were children in every sense but in their chronological age. They all loved candy and they all loved toys. So I decided to make candy and fill twelve little boxes, and to do my best to finance the purchase of twelve playthings. I explained to my relatives just why I was curtailing all other Christmas expenses except cards and stamps.

So I set to work. Does anyone know how much fudge it takes to fill twelve boxes? Batch after batch! I packed it in little plastic containers that came from the grocery store. Then I invested in a box of tangerines. I made up a concoction which as far as I know had no name. It was composed of nuts, chocolate, marshmallows, rolled oats, butter and peanut butter – a real combination. I knew they would love these, and they did.

The toys turned out to be nearly all wooly animals – lambs, lions, kittens – all warm and cuddly.

Early Christmas morning a friend drove me out to the nursing home and helped me carry all of my parcels inside. All was excitement among the patients. The nursing home owners had presented every patient with brand new underwear, which they had put on and were now parading up and down the halls, pulling up their trouser legs to show everyone their new long-johns.

I gave them the candy and they gobbled it up immediately like small children. The tangerines went fast, too. They hugged and cuddled their wooly animals, and preened themselves before the mirrors. How little it all was compared with the Christmases we were accustomed to, and yet they were delighted and blissfully happy and showed such deep appreciation that I felt a sense of shame. What had I ever done to bring joy to these people?

There was Emily, aged sixty, with the mentality of a four-year-old, found abandoned and nameless on the parish steps. Then there was Ursula, who had smallpox when she was a year old, which caused the forming of abscesses in her brain at that age. Consequently, Ursula spent her life hooking rugs and imitating bird calls, at which she was very good. And these are only two of the patients there.

This day had been a humbling experience for me as well as an exhilarating one. I revised many of my attitudes that Christmas Day.

I had to leave while the patients were having their sing-along, and as I went down the steps I was followed by their

*Notes on Ireland and Other Writings*

happy voices singing "Away in a manger, no crib for His bed............"

*Notes on Ireland and Other Writings*

## Simon Takes A Journey

The most learned physician in all Cyrenaica concluded his examination of Simon's wife, Miriam, and looked at Simon gravely. He rose, and Simon followed him out of the room. Dread was in Simon's heart.

"I wouldn't deceive you, Simon. I cannot help her. No cure has ever been found for this terrible tumor that literally eats a person alive. Thousands of people have contracted it, and all of them have died. I sometimes feel that no cure will be found for this thing ever; it has been with us since time began, and we are as helpless now as we were in the beginning." Sadly he took his leave, for Simon and Miriam were his dear friends.

Slowly Simon left the house and went into his beautiful garden. The roses might as well have been toadstools. He did not see them. He told himself, almost wonderingly, "Miriam is going to leave us. She is going to die. We will be separated forever." But he felt nothing; he was numb all over. He felt almost thankful for it, for when feeling at last returned, his grief would be too terrible to bear and live. But for now.........

181

*Notes on Ireland and Other Writings*

His two sons, Rufus, twenty, and Alexander, eighteen, came and stood beside him. Each laid a hand on his shoulder. But they said nothing; what words of comfort were there to offer?

Rufus finally broke the silence. "Father, my friend Marcus has been here and has just left. He talked once more of the great healer he met when he was in Jerusalem. He says that this healer has cured many people otherwise doomed to die. Marcus is so enthusiastic about him and says he makes the doctors look like fools."

A sad ghost of a smile touched Simon's lips. "Rufus, ever since the world began there have been healers, some good and some bad. These stories Marcus tells – they do credit to the enthusiasm of his youth, but...."

"But Father, what harm would it do to let him see Mother? I mean, I know you cancelled your trip to Jerusalem for the Passover festival on account of Mother's illness. But remember all of the doctors have said there is no cure."

"Very well," he answered wearily. "If your mother is willing to undertake the journey, ill as she is, then we will go to Jerusalem and see this miracle worker."

*Notes on Ireland and Other Writings*

Simon was a rich man, well able to provide every means of making travel easier, but that long journey to Jerusalem with a desperately sick woman was something that would probably haunt his dreams for years.

Entering the city, they found the usual crowds and excitement attendant on the Passover festival. They pressed on through the crowds towards the house of Simon's cousin. There they would stay while they remained in the city.

They were making very little progress, and Miriam seemed about to faint from exhaustion. A procession of some sort was taking place up ahead. Finally Simon stopped and said to the boys, "You two stay here with your mother while I go and see what is hindering us. We may have to find a new route."

Progress through the crowds was easier now that he was alone. Ahead he could see the procession moving slowly toward Golgotha. It was led by three criminals carrying crosses on their shoulders, presumably on their way to execution. These must be very important criminals, for a huge crowd was following them. They were guarded by watchful Roman soldiers.

As Simon was pressing forward through the crowd, a little boy tugged at his pant leg. Simon looked down and the boy said, "This man is from Bethlehem. He performs miracles. We have seen them with our own eyes." Then the boy ran off.

Simon pressed closer and for a moment his eyes met those of the man in the lead. Simon felt a sense of shock as he looked into those eyes, the eyes of One who seemed to bear all of the sorrows of the world in his heart. Criminal or not, he seemed barely able to carry he heavy cross. Suddenly he staggered, then collapsed, sinking to his knees.

The soldiers cursed him, then seeing he was unable to rise, looked around for help. The eye of one fell on Simon. He beckoned, "You there. Help him carry it. Hurry, we haven't got all day."

Simon bent and helped the man to his feet. The cross-beam of the cross was laid across his shoulders, and the procession resumed its march to the Hill of the Skull. The man touched Simon's hand and said, "Thank you for helping me. You are very kind."

Simon felt confused. He was a law-abiding man, and he believed that crime should be punished. Yet more and more

*Notes on Ireland and Other Writings*

the conviction that this man was no criminal grew within him until it filled heart and brain to almost bursting. Simon said to himself, "He is no criminal. There is a goodness in him. He is radiant with it."

Then they were there. The man turned to Simon and said quickly, "Go back now to your family. You will find that she who you thought was lost has been restored. Hurry now."

Simon found himself obeying without question. Slowly he left Golgotha and the timeless drama being enacted there. Rufus and Alexander came running to meet him. And Miriam, yes Miriam, hurrying after.

"Simon!" she exclaimed. "I don't know what happened. Suddenly I felt no pain, my strength came back, and I could stand up. It was like a miracle."

Simon's eyes gazed back to Golgotha. The crosses were now standing upright in the ground and the executions would come forthwith.

He then looked at Miriam and tears swelled in his eyes. "Yes, yes, Miriam. It is a miracle. A great and wonderful miracle."

## Zelophehad's Girls

(Editor's note: my aunt probably based this story on the characters and story in the Bible)

In a tent in an Israelite camp on the east bank of the Jordan river across from Jericho on one hot, lazy afternoon at the end of the 15th century B. C., an indignation meeting was being held by the five young daughters of Zelophehad. Zelophehad had died while they were still in the wilderness, leaving no sons, only five daughters – Milcah, Hoglah, Noah, Mahlah and Tirzah.

Mahlah ran a caressing hand over the fleece she was combing, so soft and lovely to the touch, the healing oil from the wool so soothing to her work-roughened hands. She loved the sheep in her father's flocks and made the pretty, bouncy little lambs her special care. It was going to be hard to lose them to Cousin Abiah. "But without sons," she said, "our father's flocks will go to his nearest male kin."

Young Tirzah chimed in. "Our dear, dear cousin Abiah, no less." Cousin Abiah was rich, and he wanted to be richer. For years his greedy eyes had watched the

*Notes on Ireland and Other Writings*

great flocks of his kinsman, Zelophehad, waiting.

Noah's voice held resentment. "We will have nothing. We'll just be allowed to become members of his household. I don't want to spend the rest of my life dancing attendance on Cousin Abiah."

Tirzah's voice bristled with her indignation. "It's so unfair. Just because we are girls. It's time something was done about it."

Noah laughed bitterly. "Whoever heard of a girl inheriting anything? No, we'll just have to go and live with Cousin Abiah and he'll grudge us every bite we eat and marry us off at the first chance he gets to make a profit on us. He's already got his eye on Mahlah for his darling Korah. That way he won't have to pay any bride-price, being her guardian. Leave it to him to think of that."

Hoglah and Milcah were quiet girls given to making the best of things. They offered no comment. Hoglah continued her churning and Milcah busied herself mending a long, jagged tear in the tent's side.

Mahlah thought of her father, that gentle and kindly man. Cousin Abiah had approached Zelophehad to suggest a mar-

*Notes on Ireland and Other Writings*

riage between herself and Korah, his son. Mahlah shuddered at the idea of marrying the domineering Korah. Her father had no illusions about Abiah and Korah. He had refused to even discuss the matter.

The next day Joel, whom she loved with all of her heart, had told her that his father would come that evening to broach the subject of a marriage between himself and Mahlah. "I'm fairly sure your father looks on me with favor. He has a short way with those he doesn't. I feel sure everything will work out as we want, Mahlah."

Mahlah had been certain too, for her father had asked her about her feeling for Joel. But that night, her father had suddenly cried out. His daughters had hurried to his side. He was doubled up with pain, and despite their tender ministering, he died just as the sun rose.

Everyone mourned the loss of Zelophehad. Everyone, that is, except Cousin Abiah, whose black eyes held a look of triumph.

Now they were at the mercy of their greedy cousin, and there was no way out, for it was the law. Mahlah's eyes filled with tears, for she knew how hopeless her cause had become. Everything was different now. Cousin Abiah had come with

Korah that morning to inform them formally of their situation. "The elders have consented to the marriage between you, Mahlah, and Korah. Your sisters will live in my household and make themselves useful in return for my beneficence. I will take charge of the flocks. I trust you are suitably grateful."

"Surely," Tirzah said now, "if the elders knew how our father despised and distrusted Cousin Abiah, they wouldn't let this happen."

Hoglah answered impatiently, "They have no choice. It is the law. It has always been the law, and it always will be. You might as well give up, Tirzah. The law doesn't change."

Milcah spoke up and suggested, "It might not hurt to try —."

"Oh nonsense, Milcah!" Tension was making Mahlah's usually gentle voice tart and irritable. "You know quite well that such a thing could not be done. A woman going to the elders' tent with a complaint! It just isn't done."

Tirzah said quietly, "Perhaps my older sisters know best."

However, she lay awake that night racking her thirteen-year-old brain for a solution to their desperate situation. She

*Notes on Ireland and Other Writings*

feared greatly that Cousin Abiah was going to win out. Poor Mahlah! She and Joel could never marry now. She thought of Korah, that bully. She and her sisters had always feared him. Once he had threatened her with a poisonous snake, sending her screaming in terror to her father. Zelophehad had been furious and insisted that Korah be punished. But Cousin Abiah had only laughed and said, "Boys will be boys. It is foolish to pay attention to female hysterics." I'd like to just fix him, thought peppery little Tirzah. Mahlah was her favorite sister and her mind continued to chew at Mahlah's trouble.

At last she fell into a troubled sleep, and as she slept, she dreamed – they were back in the wilderness and she saw a lamb, whose leg had been struck by some animal, lying on the ground. The elder Joshua lifted the pathetic little creature and bound the injured leg, and after that as they marched slowly northward, she watched him carrying the lamb over the weary miles.

Morning dawned and surprisingly Tirzah felt herself once more ready to face the reality of their situation. She wasted no time in argument, but simply dropped the bombshell. "I'm going to see the elders."

*Notes on Ireland and Other Writings*

"You most certainly are not," stormed Hoglah, conscious of her seniority. "You wouldn't dare!"

"Well," Tirzah admitted, "I do feel a bit squeamish about going alone. Anybody want to come along?" She looked around hopefully.

"No!" the answer came vociferously from four young throats.

"Oh, all right. I just thought I'd ask." A bit defeated, she left the tent and started down the trail to the elders' tent.

"She looks so alone," said Hoglah, an uncertain note in her voice. She thought to herself that Tirzah looked more and more like their mother every day....oh, if Mother were only with them now. She could always make things come out right.

Mahlah was thinking of Tirzah also. "She looks so little," she said. "You know what I think? I think we are a bunch of snakes." Her voice became urgent. She called after her sister. "Tirzah! Tirzah! Wait for me. I'm going with you." And she dashed down the trail after her sister.

Milcah, Noah and Hoglah stared at one another, questioningly. Then, of one accord, they began racing down the trail along with their other two sisters.

191

*Notes on Ireland and Other Writings*

And so it was that the elders found themselves staring in disbelief at the five disheveled young women standing before them. Then Joshua, ever kind and ever courteous, asked, "In what way may we serve you?"

And the story poured out. How their father had worried about their future under Cousin Abiah. How he had refused to even consider a marriage between Mahlah and Korah. How Abiah was now, as their guardian, forcing Mahlah into a marriage with his son. How he was taking possession of the great flocks of their father, thus making them dependent on his charity.

Tirzah added the finishing note. "It is so unfair. All of this is taking place simply because we are girls!"

Everyone looked shocked at such temerity, especially from a young girl. Everyone that is, except Joshua, who just smiled and said, "The point is well taken."

Then the elders went into a huddle. Protests were many and were vociferous, but at last Joshua came back to them.

"In accord with what was obviously your father's wish, you will receive your inheritance. Your kinsman will get nothing. Also, he will be removed from your guardianship and I will assume that responsibility

*Notes on Ireland and Other Writings*

myself. However, should you marry outside your own tribe, the flocks will be retained by the tribe, for it is not right that another tribe should have the benefit of them. And this will be the law from this day forward."

The Zelophehad girls were jubilant. How Mahlah could marry Joel instead of the hated Korah, and they would not have to live under Cousin Abiah's thumb.

Tirzah was very happy, but she still saw room for improvement. "Now, the next thing to do is work towards getting that phrase about marrying outside the tribe struck out and changed. We will form a Committee of Ways and Means. And we really should have a good snappy slogan. How about this, girls — women's lib is on the march!"

*Notes on Ireland and Other Writings*

## Some Memories of Frances

Frances was a small village, an old elk stamping ground, set like a shallow platter among the Willapa Hills. We moved there when I was five years old and lived there until my father died, just before my ninth birthday. The town boasted a church, a school, a town hall, a general store – and a blind pig.

There was a huge cedar stump, about two feet high and about seven feet in diameter, in our back yard, and here my sister and I delighted to hold 'tea parties.' Once my mother sent me to the store with fifty cents to buy oranges. It seemed they were out of oranges, but they had other goodies, and I was not one to pass up a bargain. When I got home I gave my mother the huge sack I was carrying.

"They were out of oranges, but just look at what I got in place of them," I said. She opened the sack and looked inside. What she saw was fifty small fluted tin dishes filled with a nougat-type candy, each and every one equipped with a mini-sized spoon. I was quite disappointed that she did not turn the whole thing over to us, but doled out two a day to my sister Nellie and

194

me. We set the table on the cedar stump for our tea parties and served the goodies along with cups of tea, which were really warm milk.

The church stood halfway up the hillside, and the cemetery extended on up the hill back of the church. Pallbearers found it hard work to carry the caskets up that steep grade from the church door. In late spring the cemetery was a sheet of white Star-of-Bethlehem blossoms which had naturalized there. Above the cemetery the hill dropped abruptly into a narrow valley, through which ran beautiful Fern Creek. To me that valley seemed the loveliest spot in the world.

At some time in history an ancient cedar tree had fallen across the creek, forming a bridge. Once when the priest took us on a nature hike, Merele Christian fell from the log into the creek. She was not badly hurt but scared, and very, very wet. The priest took us back up the bluff to the cemetery and told Merele to take off her dress and lay it across one of the granite headstones to dry. It was a hot May afternoon and the granite, hot as a stove, soon dried the dress. While we sat around waiting for it to dry the priest told us about his home in Italy, and the seven little sisters whom he had helped his mother care for. His voice was wistful and he was obviously lonely for them, and living in a strange country. It calls for a lot of self-denial to go into the priesthood.

A little way beyond the log bridge was my favorite spot. Here the current had cut into the bank, making a pool, roughly circular in shape and about fifteen feet across. In July this pool was smothered in blossoming water lilies, and on the bank, shaded by the tall trees, was a long, mossy log. The branches of some of the trees overhung the water, and it was my delight to crawl out on one of those branches and bounce it up and down. This was truly a magic place, where anything could happen, and sometimes did. Almost sixty-five years later I made this spot the setting for a children's story.

A much smaller creek, about eight or nine feet wide, ran through our back yard on its way to empty into Fern Creek. Someone had built a small raft and moored it on the bank of this creek. It was the delight of my friends Merele and Emma and I to maneuver this awkward structure up and down the stream. We had no trouble at all in transposing ourselves into intrepid and venturesome navigators on our way to the river mouth and the open sea. It just goes to show what imagination can do for you with the aid of a few props.

School, of course, was the major interest in all our lives. There were two rooms in the Catholic school, and two Sisters. The larger room held the kindergarten and the first four grades, with Sister Tecla, our beloved teacher. The desks and seats were about six or seven feet long, with three pupils at each desk. They were roomy and comfortable, with plenty of wriggling space. There were two extra sets stacked against the side wall by the water pail. Everyone had a collapsible aluminum cup to take along on visits to the water pail.

In the back of the room, high upon the wall, hung the picture of Satan. It was one of those medieval pictures, with the Devil, complete with horns and forked tail, attempting to climb up out of Hell through a furnace-like door, while an angel with a pitchfork was poking him back down where he belonged.

I loved the kindergarten class. Before I started school I had never played with other children, and to be among such a delightful group of my peers was sheer ecstasy. Shortly before Christmas Sister Tecla appeared with some 18-inch squares

of cloth, blue checked, with the checks
about the size of those in the old red and
white checked tablecloths.

"Now," she said, "we are going to make
baby-head sofa cushions for Christmas
presents." She showed us how to thread
our needles and use our thimbles. "Now,
these are made by outlining with stitches
the white squares only. When you have
outlined a square, draw up your thread
and fasten it securely. Then go on to your
next baby-head." How pretty they were,
those baby-head sofa cushions. I have
never seen one since.

One hot afternoon in May, nearly time
for the summer vacation, and with all of
us afflicted with spring fever, Sister Tecla
was called out of the room.

She was away for a long time. Finally our
restlessness found expression in speech.
After a few wisecracks, we began talking
about the Devil and how much we hated
him, and what we would do to him if we
had the chance. Someone said, "I would
spit on his picture if I could reach it. But
who could spit way up there?"

"So would I," another pupil agreed. "I
would too.....me too...." Every pupil in the
class eventually joined in. Finally, one
said, "Those extra desks........."

We all looked at the desks for a few minutes, and then it was just too much for us. With one accord we all converged on the desks, shoving them to the back of the room directly below the Devil's picture. Then, with considerable effort, we piled one desk on top of another. Then one by one, we mounted the precarious perch, and proceeded to show the Devil just what we thought of him. After everyone had been up once, we then started a second round.

Suddenly, Sister Tecla was in the room. She stood there, her face quite a study. She whacked a desk with her pointer and said, "All right. Everyone line up." Meekly, we all took our places in the line-up. She took her pointer and gave us all two good whacks on the right spot. For the rest of the afternoon you could hear a pin drop in the classroom.

Finally she said as we were about to leave, "I don't care if it is the Devil. That is not something you do."

As I started home after dismissal, I remembered that my hair ribbon had come untied and I had stuck it in my desk. I turned back and as I opened the classroom door, I saw Sister Tecla and the other Sister standing below the Devil's pic-

*Notes on Ireland and Other Writings*

ture, and they were both speechless with laughter.

Bellingham, Washington
June 17, 1977

*Notes on Ireland and Other Writings*

## Mr. Holland's Inheritance

The lawyer's keen eye traveled slowly over the figure before him, missing no details of the scuffed, thin-soled shoes, the somewhat threadbare gray suit and the hat which had obviously seen more prosperous days. He also noted the somewhat discouraged droop of the shoulders. He mentally summed up the young man as another of the fast swelling army of the unemployed.

Aloud he said, "It seems, Mr. Holland, that your grandfather has left you this property on condition that you occupy it immediately for a period of one year. The property consists entirely of a small hospital located in Bantonville, up on the Canadian border I believe. In addition to this, you were to receive the sum of two hundred dollars, payable immediately."

Frank Holland sat very still for a few moments. Then he asked, "This hospital – is it in use now?"

"No," was the reply. "It isn't. I suppose the thing for you to do, if you want to put it on a paying basis, is to lease it to a physician. I understand it is still equipped for use as a hospital."

*Notes on Ireland and Other Writings*

"I haven't a thing in the world to keep me in New York," mused Holland. "I suppose I could leave tomorrow. I'll just take that two hundred and we'll consider this deal on. I'd rather spend a year in the hospital than a year on a park bench."

A couple of days later Frank Holland arrived in Bantonville. His first requirement, he felt, was to satisfy the inner man. He made his way to the town's one restaurant.

After he had taken the wise edge off his appetite, he began to take note of his surroundings. There was no one except himself at the lunch counter, and the combination cook and waiter began to exhibit a desire to be sociable.

"Stranger here, aren't ye?" he asked. "Are ye planning to settle down here for a spell?"

"Yes," was the reply. "I'm planning to make my home in the Holland hospital. I'm the new owner. My name is Holland."

The effect of these words on the other man was somewhat surprising. He dropped the second cup of coffee on the floor that Holland had ordered and stared as if he had taken leave of his senses.

202

*Notes on Ireland and Other Writings*

"You – you mean you're figurin' on spending your nights in that place?" he shrilled.

"Why, is the place so badly out of repair?" asked Holland, somewhat amused.

"Out of repair?" snorted the other man. "I should say it is. But that isn't all. There's mighty queer goings-on at night up there in that place. You take my advice and give it a good wide berth."

"But why?" Holland persisted. "What is going on there? If it's anything serious it seems that it would be the owner's responsibility to investigate."

"Well, I know I wouldn't stick my head in that place after nightfall. I have seen and heard strange things."

"Where is the building? Can you see it from here?" Holland asked.

"Yes, of course. Just come over here to the door and you get a pretty good view of it."

As Holland joined him in the doorway, he resumed. "You see that old wooden building upon the side of the hill. The back of the building is smack up against the Canadian line. They scooped out half the side of the hill and built the hospital up against the side of the cliff. Funny shape, that hill is. A very high, narrow ridge."

*Notes on Ireland and Other Writings*

Holland consulted his watch and it was not yet five o'clock. He told the other man that he would go up and look at the place at least.

"You're crazy, darn crazy I tell you," sputtered the other man, whose name in the conversations had been revealed as Clem Robinson. "We're going to have a thunderstorm in the course of an hour or two. See them clouds."

Holland persisted in his intention however, and he presently took leave of Mr. Robinson and started up the long road that wound up the side of the hill.

\* \* \* \*

Frank Holland stood gazing at his inheritance for one long, disillusioned moment. In that time his belief that he possessed a source of income passed into the realm of lost hopes. Blankly, the broken fan light over the entrance stared back at him as if questioning his presence in a place ordinarily shunned by men. It was an ancient wooden structure, and badly in need of paint. All the windows had been boarded up. The fan light gave the place the appearance of a disreputable, one-eyed old man.

*Notes on Ireland and Other Writings*

Holland's thoughts were in chaos. Only the realization that he had nothing to lose prevented him from turning around in disgust.

Finally he decided to go around to the back, as efforts to open the front door with the key the lawyer had given him proved fruitless. Here a mild surprise awaited him. There was a wood pile by the back door, with wood that had been split. Idly he tried the door knob, and to his surprise it opened immediately. "Why isn't the back door locked?" he asked himself. It was like someone had been there recently.

The back door opened directly into the kitchen. Here he found a range, cooking utensils, coffee and sundry other cooking supplies.

On a sudden impulse he decided to go back to the village and procure some bacon and eggs and cook his supper on the range. He was almost on his way down the hill when the thought had formed.

The storm broke while he was in town. It broke with such violence that for a moment he was tempted to give it up and spend the night in town. The temporary spurt of fear went away and soon he was climbing his way back up the hill with his purchases.

By the time he reached the kitchen again he was drenched, and the fire, which he had started in the range before he left, was very welcome.

After he had dined he lit his pipe and proceeded to make an exploratory tour of the building. There was no electricity but he found several powerful flashlights in the cupboard over the sink, and took one of these instead of the kerosene lamp on the kitchen table.

The downstairs part of the building, with the exception of the kitchen, was totally unfurnished. But upstairs the first door he opened revealed a bed, obviously left untouched from the time when it had been used as a hospital cot. There were a number of built-in cupboards in the room, evidently used to hold hospital supplies or patients' clothing.

He opened several doors leading off from the corridor, but the rooms were almost uniform in their sameness.

He was just closing the fifth door when his flashlight picked up something dark on the floor on the opposite side of the bed. He moved closer. It was a foot, projecting a few inches from under the bed.

Quick as a flash, Holland had dragged from under the bed a wriggling, squirming

*Notes on Ireland and Other Writings*

figure. Then he gaped in surprise. The figure that was cowering before him was a girl, with a rather pale face streaked with tears and rather pathetic looking.

Holland finally found his voice, and rather strong at that. "May I inquire, young lady, who you are and just how you came to be under that bed?"

The young girl had to catch her breath for a moment too, for she also was surprised at a man suddenly coming in to where she slept.

She finally spoke. "Are you Mr. Holland?"

He was rather taken aback. "Uh....yes, I am....how do you know me?"

"My name is Jane Riverton. I came up from San Francisco over a week ago. My father was a business associate of your grandfather. My parents have divorced and neither one could care for me, and I heard something about a property near the Canadian border. When I got into town I went to see the lawyer and he told me where the property was. I had nowhere else to go so I came here. I didn't want to disturb the beds or anything so I just slept on the floor. I am sorry."

Holland swallowed and thought a moment before replying. "You realize this is not your property?"

*Notes on Ireland and Other Writings*

"Yes, I do," the girl replied. "I came here and no one was here, so I thought it was deserted and that no one was tending to it. I am sorry, Mr. Holland."

Holland gazed out the window. "Oh, it's ok," he replied, then looked at her. "You look hungry."

"Yes, oh yes," Jane replied. "I haven't eaten since breakfast the day before yesterday. Didn't I smell coffee and bacon cooking a while back?"

Without replying, Holland dashed out of the room and back to the kitchen, where he replenished the waning fire. Then he busied himself with making fresh coffee, slicing bacon and stirring up eggs for an omelet.

When these were cooked to a turn Holland sent the word 'chow' reverberating through the empty corridors, and within a few seconds the girl was sitting at the kitchen table. She ate as if half-starved, yet there was an innate daintiness about her which appealed to Holland.

When she had finished the last slice of bacon and drained the coffee pot, she leaned back in her chair and surveyed her host with considerable interest and curiosity. Evidently she was pleased with her scrutiny, for she spoke in a much more

208

*Notes on Ireland and Other Writings*

friendly voice and manner than she did before.

"I suppose you are wondering what to do with me or how to rid yourself of me," she said. "But as I mentioned, I really have no other place to go."

"You are welcome to stay here as long as you like," answered Holland. "I understand you have no other place to go."

As they continued talking, it was revealed that Jane was the person who had cut the wood. With her milling about the building and property at night, she was also probably the source of the "strange things" that Clem Robinson had seen and heard.

They spent the day going around the building and trying to spruce it up any way they could. Holland had been thinking the whole day also.

Finally he turned to Jane and asked, "If you have nowhere to go and no one to take care of you, would you mind if I adopted you and took you as my own? If I turn this place into a hospital again or whatever I decide to do, I won't be alone, and you won't be alone."

"That would be very nice, Mr. Holland." Jane Riverton was pleased. "I would like that very much. I don't know what to do with this place, but maybe something. If not we will most certainly figure out something else. I believe we both have industrious minds."

The next morning they went into town and talked with the lawyer, and the lawyer set into motion the process for Mr. Holland to adopt the girl.

That night in bed, Mr. Holland stared up at the ceiling. He came out here not knowing what to expect. He first saw the building and had been disillusioned. But there was a girl who would soon become his with the adoption. You never know what will happen in life or what will be around the next corner. All in all, quite an inheritance.

*Notes on Ireland and Other Writings*

# Tillicum

(Editor's note: This story was previously published in the book "Spoken In Due Season" from the Writing Class at the Senior Activity Center in Bellingham, Washington. It was edited by Dorothy Koert and published in 1979.)

\*   \*   \*   \*

When I was about five years old, we moved to Frances, a small village in Washington, set in a shallow bowl in the midst of the Willapa Hills. It was, we were told, the location of a very ancient elk stamping ground. The subject interested my parents and I heard it discussed many times during the following months.

The thought of those thousands of elk gripped my imagination, which was a fer tile one, always on the alert for something new to explore. And so it was that my imaginary elk emerged, part legend, part history, part fantasy, and to me, wholly fascinating.

He was a wonderful friend. He stood head and shoulders above the rest of the herd. His eyes were a lovely, glowing brown, like

*Notes on Ireland and Other Writings*

dark amber. And I named him 'Tillicum' which is an Indian word meaning 'friend.'

The first time we met, we eyed each other warily. Then I said, "Are you one of the ancient elk who lived here?"

He replied, and I had no trouble understanding him. "Of course, I am. And this is the rest of the herd."

Then I saw that more and more elk were appearing here and there. They just seemed to materialize out of thin air, more and more of them, until they became an army. And then the houses of the town began to shrink until they were like doll houses and quite transparent, so you could see inside them. I stuck an experimental finger down Mr. Handy's chimney and it stuck there. I had a real struggle to pull it free, and meanwhile the huge elk waited.

Free at last, I turned to him. "But you have been dead for centuries. Your bones lie buried deep under the earth here."

"Yes," he replied, "that is true. But that is only our *bones. We* are here all the time, but only certain people can see us. Mostly, when humans get their first glimpse of us, they refuse to believe their eyes, and we immediately become invisible to them." He tossed his beautiful head. "We don't force

*Notes on Ireland and Other Writings*

ourselves on anyone. But the ones who have eyes to see will *see*."

He turned to the herd, which had been milling about, nibbling grass, pretending to nip each other's heels and other antics. But now they saw their leader waiting for their attention and they quickly came into military formation.

He addressed them, "It is now time for our daily stamping drill. We will be joined today by our young friend here."

He turned courteously to me, "She will undoubtedly find it interesting."

Interesting! I was thrilled to death, and he called, "One, two, three, stamp! One, two, three, stamp! One, two, three, stamp! And the thunder of their stamping echoed and re-echoed through the Willapa Hills, and came back to us like the rolling music of beating drums.

Tillicum and I had many wonderful adventures that summer. Whenever I thought of him, he would appear. There was a bit of mystery about his appearances. I never actually saw him come, or saw him go, he was just *there*. This did not seem unnatural to me at the time, nor did the manner in which the houses in the village became tiny and transparent whenever he was there. The surrounding

213

forests on the hills came much closer, so they hemmed in the stamping ground.

The last time I saw him, he carried me on his great shoulders far away over the hills to the seashore, traveling over the treetops with the speed of the wind. I had never been to the sea and the roar of the breakers shattering on the rocks was a wonderful sound – like organ music.

We rested on the sandy beach. Being more curious than usual, I asked, "Tillicum, how did you do that – travel over the treetops, I mean?"

He said nothing for a moment, and when he looked at me his eyes were very sad. "Have you forgotten how it is? Yesterday you *knew* these things, and never questioned them. Are you beginning to doubt?"

"How do you come so strangely?" I persisted. "One moment you are not there, and then – there you are."

But he did not answer my questions. "Come. It is late and you must be home before dark." I mounted his great shoulders and away we went, like the wind. I went to sleep before we arrived, and when I awoke again, I was in my own bed and it was morning.

*Notes on Ireland and Other Writings*

Tillicum never came again. I tried many times to bring him to me by fixing my thoughts on him, but he was lost to me.

More than sixty-five years have passed since that wonderful summer. A year ago I went back to Frances. Should one ever go back? Some say it is a mistake. I don't know. The village had changed very little. The wooded hills still encircled it.

*Did* a ghostly herd of ancient elk still mill about on the old stamping ground? Surely that was a magnificent antlered head looking at me from under the trees. But of course not! It was only the gnarled, age-whitened roots of an uprooted cedar. I was a grown woman now, too wise for such childish fantasies. I could see nothing now but the trees. And yet —, and yet —??

*Notes on Ireland and Other Writings*

## The Moon and Ellen Adele

(Editor's note: This story was previously published in the book "Spoken In Due Season" from the Writing Class at the Senior Activity Center in Bellingham, Washington. It was edited by Dorothy Koert and published in 1979.)

\*   \*   \*   \*

"Moon, please let me find you and hold you close," said Ellen Adele, who had been named for her grandmother, who died when Ellen Adele was a baby. She had always known that Grandmother had been in love with the moon, too.

When she was born, Grandmother had made her a tiny teddy bear, eight inches tall, from an old red flannel petticoat. Ellen Adele had fallen in love with Teddy, so bravely red, with shoe button eyes. She played with him constantly. Eventually he lost one of his shoe button eyes and some of the stuffing came out of his neck, so that his head sagged on his chest like that of a hanged man. Then when she was about a year old, Teddy disappeared.

Teddy was in her thoughts now, as she stood at her bedroom window at midnight. The full August moon cast a long shadow of the spruce tree over the front porch. "Whatever could have happened to my red teddy bear?" It has not been seen since the morning Grandpa went away.

Yesterday she had asked her father about Grandpa, "Why did he leave us, Daddy? Won't he come home again, ever?"

Daddy's face was sober. "Well, Darling, after Grandma died, he grieved. He would sit for hours staring at nothing. He had a lost look. Then, one morning he packed a few things and told us he was leaving. Going in search of Grandma's moon. Don't look for letters," he told us, "I don't know what the future holds. When I find a way to pick up my life again, then I'll come home!"

Shortly after that the company transferred Daddy to the west coast. He left his address with friends who promised to forward any letters from Grandpa. No letters ever came.

Ellen sighed, "It will be simply wonderful if he ever comes home. He'd tell me about the Moon Lady who was Grandma." Yesterday she had asked, "What did Grandma look like, Daddy?"

He took her to the mirror. "When you grow up, you will probably look just like her. *You* are a Moon Lady too, you know."

Tonight the moon was enticing, beckoning her irresistibly. "How wonderful it would be, to hold it, cradle it, in my arms."

The moon was calling, calling. She must answer the call. Putting on her bathrobe and bedroom slippers, she slipped quietly down the stairs and out the front door. On the dusty road she stood motionless for a moment, hands clasped beseechingly. "Moon, please, please, let me find you and hold you tight in my arms. Tighter than tight!"

At first the walking was easy. The yellow dust, three inches deep in a dry summer, got into her slippers and sifted through the feet of her Denton Sleepers. It felt nice, like walking in Mother's face powder. She wondered what Mother would say when she saw the dirty feet of those Denton Sleepers. But that was for tomorrow. Now, Ellen trudged on, but the roadway now was full of small pebbles, which kept getting into her slippers. They hurt and made her feet sore. Finally, she was forced to sit down and remove the slippers. She placed them neatly side by side at the edge of the road. "I'll pick them up when I come back with the moon," she told herself.

It was easier after that, though she was becoming very tired and hungry. The moon still looked as far away as ever, just above the hill. "But the hill isn't any closer, either," she thought. Suddenly, far ahead, she saw a light. Hurrying toward it, she could see a small campfire at the edge of the cedar grove flanking the road. Two men sat by the fire, and they were eating something that smelled absolutely delicious. Her mouth watered. The long walk had really given her an appetite. One of the men was small, with flaming red hair which bushed out in all directions. The other man was very thin and wore a long, gray beard. His eyes were kind and rather sad.

Ellen Adele felt no fear. After watching for a moment, she walked over to the fire. The two stared at her, wide-eyed and speechless. Finally the bearded man said, "Who are you? Why are you out at this hour, little girl?"

"My name is Ellen Adele," she answered. "It's after my grandmother." She was silent, hesitant. Finally she spoke. "I know who *you* are. You're God, aren't you?"

The bearded man looked at her strangely. "No, Ellen Adele. I am only a chaser of moonbeams."

"I love the moon, too," she told him. "Grandmother loved the moon. Grandpa used to call her 'Moon Lady.' I'm looking for the moon tonight. Can you help me find it? I want to hug it, tighter than tight."

The bearded man's voice was husky. "Little Ellen Adele, I have followed that moon for too many years. All I've learned is that no man can grasp it. But hold out your hands, cupped like this." He took her two hands and held them, showing her. "Now, see? The moon has filled them full and overflowing with her beams. Your hands are bathed in her radiance. Accept her gift with grace and humility. But she cannot leave her ordained place in the heavens."

Suddenly Ellen Adele was very happy. She understood now about the moon and sat contentedly cuddling moonbeams in her hands and smiling. She looked up at the man, "What is that you are eating?"

"It's beans, Ellen Adele. Would you like some?" He spooned beans into an empty tomato can and handed them to her, along with a fat wiener. She finished the beans and yawned suddenly, then yawned again.

*Notes on Ireland and Other Writings*

It had been a long day. And suddenly, she was asleep.

She was awakened by the sound of men's voices coming toward her. Suddenly Daddy was there, and the sheriff and some other men. The campfire was cold ashes now and her two friends were gone. They had covered her from the falling dew with an old gunny sack.

Daddy held her close, gunny sack and all. "Darling, why did you run away? We would never have known where to look for you if we hadn't found your slippers."

"I went to find the moon, Daddy. But I found God instead, and He explained to me about the moon. But Daddy, why did God go away?"

"I don't know, dear. But you know God has an awful lot of little girls to look after. Perhaps that is why He had to go. What's this you are holding so carefully under your gunny sack?" He drew out the small object, and suddenly Daddy was very still. He was staring at a bedraggled, one-eyed teddy bear, once bravely red, fashioned from an old-fashioned red flannel petticoat.

# THE INNKEEPER'S CHILD

Eight-year-old Claudia watched the woman riding the little donkey with a twinge of sympathy tugging at her heart. The man leading the donkey looked very weary also. Claudia laid aside her painting; it was becoming too dark anyway. Her curiosity was piqued by the pair approaching her father's inn through the snow. It promised to be a bitterly cold night, and the little donkey worked his way through to the inn.

Putting on her heavy coat, Claudia went to meet the pair. Jonathan, her innkeeper father, waited just inside the door, watching his young daughter Claudia walking towards him with the travelers. Claudia, he thought, had the elegant gait of her patrician Roman mother. But her face mirrored also the warmth and earthi-

*Notes on Ireland and Other Writings*

ness of the humble of the world. She certainly did not get that from his wife Julia.

Claudia stood by the entrance now, as the middle-aged, kindly looking man helped the very weary young woman down from the donkey's back. She pleaded their case.

"Dear Father, they have come so far, all the way from Nazareth, for the taxing. Can you not find room for them here? They have tried everywhere, but the taxing has brought so many travelers."

Claudia listened while Jonathan talked to the quiet-voiced man about lodging for the night. He seemed dubious, but Claudia knew there was one room left.

"I don't know what to say," the innkeeper said. "The only room we have left.... my wife Julia thinks that one high in the king's favor will be coming tonight, and she wants the room unoccupied. I'm sorry. And it doesn't look like you have much chance of finding lodging anywhere else tonight, either. This taxing business has upset our whole system of living. But I don't know what I can do."

The young woman drooped with exhaustion and sighed. Claudia could see her father weakening. He looked at her for moral support, and she smiled and

*Notes on Ireland and Other Writings*

nodded her encouragement. Heaven help them when Julia found out about it.

"Thinking it over," said Jonathan, "I believe I can let you have the room."

The man thanked him, and added, "My betrothed Mary is pregnant as well." His wife smiled in friendly fashion, but before she could speak Julia stormed into the room. Jonathan gulped, and Claudia lowered her eyes.

Claudia's beautiful Roman mother gazed over the couple, then towards Jonathan, then towards Claudia, and finally looked at the strangers coldly.

"These people," Julia's diction was more faultless than usual when she wanted to show disdain, "these people will have to go elsewhere. We have no more room. I myself assigned the big room facing the garden to a gentleman who has all the requirements of prestige."

Jonathan swallowed hard and then replied, "I just gave them the big room facing the garden, my dear."

Annoyance reddened her cheeks and sparked her eyes. She answered, "Jonathan...you know very well I have been saving the big room. What am I to do when the royal guest arrives. They will

*Notes on Ireland and Other Writings*

have to go elsewhere. That is all there is to it."

"But, my dear," replied Jonathan, "there are no other rooms anywhere around. And the young woman is about due to have a child."

"It isn't our responsibility to house every foot-traveler who passes our way," Julia responded. She believed that common people should be nipped in the bud. These people certainly appeared common, though respectable.

The weary traveler Joseph broke in. "It's quite all right. Come, Mary, we must hurry if we are to find a place tonight."

As Mary slowly followed Joseph out the door, Claudia spoke up. "Father, would it be okay if they stayed in the stable? We can't just turn them away in the cold and snow. I am sure there are no rooms anywhere around."

Jonathan glanced at Julia. Julia gave no response and walked out of the room. So it was decided that the weary travelers would stay in the stable.

\*     \*     \*     \*

Julia was the daughter of Marcus, a great painter, as well as the friend and protégé of the Roman emperors. Jonathan was the son of a well-to-do Jewish scholar. He desired to become a painter, though he had no talent for it. But his father was financially able to indulge his son's wish, so Jonathan became the pupil of Marcus.

Jonathan had mistaken his appreciation of art for talent, and Marcus soon wearied of his bargain.

Meanwhile, Marcus' daughter Julia had fallen in love with Jonathan, and he with her. Marcus was opposed to a marriage between them, but he was also no match for his daughter in a contest of wills. Eventually she wore him down, and he gave his consent.

Shortly after they were married, Jonathan's father lost his wealth, and as a painter he was a fizzle. His dreaminess and idealism were against him as he could find no career for which he was suitably fitted.

Finally he became an innkeeper, and it was into this circumstance that their daughter Claudia was born. From the hour of her birth Julia's every effort was bent toward the goal of restoring her daughter to the station in life her parents had been forced to abandon.

*Notes on Ireland and Other Writings*

The very thing that had appealed to her about Jonathan at the time of their marriage was now what gave her such frustration. Being Roman to her fingertips, she was a practical woman. What was perfectly proper for them to do and feel when they were wealthy was the utmost of folly in these circumstances. She felt that hospitality was a luxury for the rich, and the wildest extravagance for the less fortunate to indulge in.

*   *   *   *

Claudia and her father Jonathan were having a conversation when they heard Julia coming into the room. Muttering something about needing enough wine for the guests, he quickly left the room. His wife's penetrating eye followed him.

"Claudia, my dear, I have no regrets about marrying your father and coming to this uncouth country. Nonetheless, from the day you were born I dedicated my life to getting your father to go to Rome to live. You are entitled to the advantages of a cultured and civilized world and that is what I want for you."

*Notes on Ireland and Other Writings*

"If we were to go to Rome, Mother, would we live with Grandfather?" Claudia queried.

"Possibly. Though I don't think a great artist like my father would be overjoyed at the presence of a Jewish innkeeper in his home. Even so, when he found I had decided to marry your father, he realized right away that further squirming was useless. But after that his attitude toward your father left nothing to be desired."

Claudia looked at her tall beautiful mother. The lines of her flowing garment flowed smooth, relentless rhythm from shoulder to ankle. Her mother aimed at perfection in every detail of her life and the lives of those with whom she concerned herself.

Aloud Claudia said, "Come, Mother. Come see my new painting. Tell me what you think."

She led her mother to the painting that she had been putting the finishing touches on when the couple from Nazareth had asked for lodging.

Her mother gave it her thoughtful but impersonal consideration.

"It doesn't really say anything," she said. "It's pretty meaningless."

"I know," Claudia despaired. "I feel that way too."

228

*Notes on Ireland and Other Writings*

Julia looked at her daughter. "Next time, I would suggest a live subject to paint. It always seems so much more worthwhile."

Julia continued to study the painting, her eyes narrowed in concentration. She complimented her daughter.

"My child, the overall painting does leave much to be desired, but you are sheer genius when it comes to using your blues. This blue shadow is brilliant. Who else would think so? My father would. His paintings all show the same trait."

She permitted a seldom used tenderness to infuse her crisp voice with warmth. "I've tried to teach you everything he taught me. You have the gift he prayed for me to have. I think I was a bitter disappointment to him as an artist, and a puzzle with no answer as a daughter."

Julia mused for a moment, thoughts far away. Then she added, "But wait until he sees my daughter. Claudia, there is to be no early marriage for you. One way or another, you will go to your grandfather in Rome and study under him. He is a friend of the emperor. There's nothing he can't do for you, my child."

"But Mother," replied Claudia, "I have no wish to leave you and Father. You both are so good to me."

229

*Notes on Ireland and Other Writings*

Julia's brief flash of sentiment had dissipated. "Ridiculous. Whoever heard of turning your back on such a prospect. Sometimes I think you are as lacking in ambition for the honors of this world as your poor father is. Why, if I wasn't behind him, prodding him every step of the way, we'd soon be beggars in the street. Life is about gathering honors and riches and power, and as much of them as possible."

Julia looked at Claudia and smiled secretly in her heart, but her face did not move. She thought that this daydreaming would not do. She must give the girl a task every day, and also speak to her about some of her associations. From now on, she must cease her nonsensical friendships with social nobodies, like those two from Nazareth that just came. In Julia's mind, Claudia must begin to cultivate people who can be of some use to her.

Claudia was curious about her grandfather and life in Rome. After a simple life at the inn, such grandeur would be wonderful.

"Has he a very big house?" Claudia queried to her mother.

"He has a great house, many times larger than this inn," Julia replied. "In fact, you almost might call it a palace. And, in the

*Notes on Ireland and Other Writings*

garden, there is a fountain which sprays water all the time. Water is very plentiful there and does not have to be saved. If your grandfather is pleased with you, he will undoubtedly present you to the emperor, who is also his friend and patron."

"The emperor? You mean the Roman emperor?" Claudia exclaimed. "Oh, Mother, that's marvelous. How thrilling. I must tell all my friends that I am to meet the emperor when I go to Rome."

"But just a minute, Claudia," cautioned Julia. "I said your grandfather would present you to the emperor if he was pleased with you."

"I don't understand your meaning, Mother."

"My dear, your grandfather has a very strong sense of social custom." Julia looked directly at her daughter. He was not happy when I married your father, who was a mere innkeeper, and therefore socially his inferior. I do not think he would approve your friendship with such people as this couple who came to the inn this evening."

\* \* \* \*

On the night Jesus was born, Joseph and Mary were in the stable, and one of the king's nobles had arrived with his entourage. Claudia's father sent her from the room from where they were feasting.

Dejected, the girl sat at her window and thought of the travelers. How weary the woman had looked, and the man so concerned for her. She wished desperately that there had been room in the inn, but with the king and his entourage, that made it impossible to find quarters in the inn.

Suddenly she notices that the yard around the stable is full of shepherds. There is a strange light which seems to be coming from the great star above. She had never seen that star before, and it seemed to be right above the stable. How odd, she thought.

She decides to investigate, and call upon the man and woman in the stable. Before leaving she asks herself, "What have I to make their lot easier?" She selected several items from her possessions, and also filled a basket with food. Finally, she picked up her sketchbook and went on with the basket and other items to the stable.

Somewhat timidly, the innkeeper's child Claudia entered the stable. It seemed strangely bright and was very crowded. There were three richly dressed and wise looking men there besides the shepherds.

*Notes on Ireland and Other Writings*

The animals seemed different too, and looked as if it would be not difficult at all for them to speak. Everyone was looking at a tiny, beautiful newborn baby lying in a manger. The woman hovered above the manger.

The shepherds moved closer to the door, and the three wise-looking men grouped closer to Joseph who was folding his heavy robe. The young woman picked up the baby from the manger, waiting for Joseph to complete the task. When the robe is folded to his satisfaction he places it in the empty manger over some straw. After patting the robe, the mother Mary placed the child in the manger, covering part of him with the robe.

Mary turned to young Claudia and said, "I believe this child will be King one day." Claudia is enchanted by the graciousness and beauty of this young woman. They become friends, and Mary and Joseph permit Claudia to paint the scene in the stable.

The young girl stared in awe for a moment. A glowing white light illuminated the scene, possibly from the star above. She suddenly felt free of the encumbering shyness that came to a child among strange elders. She walked up to the infant and

*Notes on Ireland and Other Writings*

it raised its arms, and she picked it up. She felt so happy, and at the same time so sad, that it seemed she could not bear it. She laid the baby down once more and prepared to paint its portrait.

As Claudia painted, Mary talked to her. "It seems very barren here compared to our Galilee country. Everything grows there."

Claudia paused and answered, "I have an aunt in Nazareth. She is trying to persuade my father to move there. She says he will completely regain his health. I wish we would, especially for his sake."

She worked all night to paint that scene in her sketchbook. Finally satisfied, and very tired, she closed the sketchbook and went back to the inn.

\*     \*     \*     \*

Shortly afterward though, a messenger arrived to say that Herod has ordered all infants to be killed. The little family in the stable decides to attempt a journey down to Egypt. The three wise men, who had previously been invited by Herod to return and tell him of the Messiah, prudently decide to return to their homes by another route. Joseph and Mary manage to escape, and all of the other babies are slain.

*Notes on Ireland and Other Writings*

Claudia and her father were in despair, but Julia, with her true Roman practicality, set herself to save her infant son Dismas. She succeeded in always concealing him from Herod's soldiers. But realizing that sooner or later he would probably be discovered, it was determined to move him out of Herod's jurisdiction.

Soon Jonathan sold the inn at Bethlehem and bought one at Nazareth. Five years later, Julia dies. Soon after that Mary and Joseph return from Egypt, with Jonathan and Claudia already settled there. Claudia had hoped that the superior climate in Nazareth would help her father's health and lameness. But though she was in Nazareth, Claudia wanted to go to Jerusalem and Bethlehem, and told her father of her upcoming plans.

Claudia and Mary again met, and each successive meeting cemented their friendship. Claudia has been persuaded by Mary that Jesus is the coming King or Messiah.

And the two small children, Mary's child Jesus and Claudia's small brother Dismas, also became friends. This was rather strange because the two could not be more opposite. Even as a child Jesus was serene and a peaceful one, while Dismas was prone to sudden, violent, but

*Notes on Ireland and Other Writings*

soon over, explosions of temper. He was not a quarrelsome child however. But when the two boys would start a project, Dismas was impatient of obstacles and reacted violently and with sudden, often disastrous results to their cause. But the two boys were great friends nonetheless. Never dreaming, no doubt, that the difference in their methods would come between them in manhood, until that last moment when they both met death on the cross.

After Mary had confided to Claudia the secret of her son's identity, and even sometimes when Claudia would look at the boy or be near the boy, she felt a sudden infusion of faith and healing. The old dread of violence and of the unknown were for the moment gone. Claudia chose her course and pursued it to the very end, and found her torment gone and faith never wavering.

\* \* \* \*

Shortly after returning to Nazareth, Joseph wanted to show Mary and Jesus some caves he found as a child on Mt. Hermon. Jesus had wanted to see them for some time. Mary was not looking forward to such a journey, especially up a mountain, but she agreed to go.

"Where are these caves?" Mary asked.

"They are about one-third of the way up the northwest side of the mountain," replied Joseph as they made their way north.

Joseph looked up at the sky. No storms brewing yet. It was autumn and the heavy snows were about to come. This was about the latest in the year that such a journey should be made, without putting oneself in peril.

Mary was becoming tired, so Joseph and Jesus stopped to rest, and they had some fruit. Mary saw a peak in the distance and asked, "Is that the mountain?"

"Yes it is," Joseph replied. "We are making very good time. Not very far now."

Reaching the base of the mountain, the three turned towards the northwest corner of the base. Eventually Joseph found a fairly gradual slope to climb, so he led the other two up the mountain.

Easily the most timid and cautious of the three, Mary became apprehensive. "What if we run into robbers or hoodlums? What if wild animals or snakes are in the caves?"

Joseph looked back at her and smiled. "It's okay, Mary. I'll be careful. We will watch our steps."

*Notes on Ireland and Other Writings*

About a third of the way up the mountain, the path turned and went sharply upward. Then it somewhat flattened out in the side of the mountain. About fifty feet away, under a narrow and low overhang, was the tiny opening to a cave.

"There is the first cave!" Joseph exclaimed. "Just as I remember. The path continues and there are more caves."

Mary wanted to rest for the evening, as it was growing dark.

"Okay, Mary." Joseph agreed. "We will rest here and be on our way back to Nazareth tomorrow."

Mary looked at Jesus, who was busy exploring every inch of the cave wall and interior. She still believed that he would be King someday. Before she went to sleep, she found a small stone tablet and inscribed a message on the tablet. Then she wrapped animal hide around the tablet, rolled it up, and placed it along the cave wall. Shortly afterward, all three were asleep.

The next morning, they retraced their steps back down the mountain and arrived in Nazareth late in the day.

"Thank you for taking us to the caves," Jesus said. "What an adventure."

"You are welcome," replied Joseph.

*Notes on Ireland and Other Writings*

\*　　\*　　\*　　\*

Before departing for Jerusalem and Bethlehem, Claudia was telling Mary and Jesus of her impending journey. She also talked often with the young Jesus about his birthplace. She told him about wanting to visit old friends and relatives who lived in houses near their former inn. She says it was from these people that she had procured Snowflake, her present to Jesus on his birthday, since some of them raised the much prized pigeons. Jesus finally asked her if she would take the pigeon with her to Bethlehem, and have the boy that raised the pigeon send him a letter. He also asked her to bring back a pigeon from Bethlehem, so that he may send that pigeon back with a message. These things she agreed to do.

Her visit to Jerusalem was short and without incident. Upon arriving in Bethlehem for a visit, Claudia was in center of town with her friends and told of a child who had escaped the massacre of the infants, and that she had painted his picture along with his parents. She added that the child's mother had said he was the Messiah.

On her final day in Bethlehem, while she was eating in the kitchen, her friends huddled outside. They decided to send a warning note by carrier pigeon back to Nazareth. A few hours later, Claudia said goodbye to everyone and left.

Sending the warning note was a good idea. The information Claudia had shared in town had been overheard by one of the king's spies, who went hastily back to his ruler. The Herod of the massacre was dead, but the current ruler, hearing of the escaped child, became fearful for the sanctity of his throne.

He stood before his chief advisor, some soldiers in his army and the spy and thundered, "If this girl has a picture of the child's parents, they can be recognized and the child can be found and slain. Go, and bring me this young woman – alive – so that she may be questioned, and bring her painting also."

Claudia arrives home to find Joseph at the door with Snowflake, the carrier pigeon. The bird bears a message from her former host. It says that the king's soldiers had come to arrest her and when they found her gone, had returned to their ruler. It was to be feared that she would be pursued and brought back. Suspicion rose that her telling of the painting and of Jesus' escape had been overheard and taken to the king by one of the paid spies, who were always milling about.

Claudia went to the window and just stared for a moment, deep in thought.

Joseph came over to her. "I want to help you. And you need not try to protect us or Jesus."

Claudia finally stopped staring and looked at him. "Nobody around the king knows what you or Jesus looks like. I have the painting which shows that and now they know about it. If you help me you would be in danger just like me."

She decides to leave Nazareth at once and make her way to Damascus. Her grandfather, a great Roman painter and close friend of the Roman emperor, is in Damascus painting pictures for the emperor's palace there. Claudia hopes to win him to her cause and through him reach the ear of the emperor.

After hearing her explain and hearing of the warning message, Claudia's father Jonathan is fearful for her but she is determined to try. She feels that the emperor might even accept the painting for his palace where it will hang forever, for the world to see.

"My dear girl," Jonathan said, "this is madness, sheer madness, to undertake a journey like that. Do you know how far Damascus is? And to be in danger of being captured and carried off to the king's torture chambers at any moment. No, Claudia. I beg you. Destroy the painting and go into hiding for awhile. We can hide you where you won't be found."

Claudia stopped and faced him. "Dear Father." She touched his hand quickly and tenderly. "You've always been so kind, so understanding. Please try to understand now, and forgive my leaving."

Her voiced faltered as she said this, for she realized that the course before her seemed so full of hazards unseen and unanticipated. But she managed to turn back to her father and continue.

"Father, this portrait is something that the world will want to receive one day. My grandfather, after I tell him the story of Jesus, will realize that he is the Messiah. I know he will. Then he can use his influence with the emperor to offer Jesus his protection. And the portrait will be there for those who want to see."

She put on her heavy coat, and placed her portrait in an inside pocket that she had sewn. She gathered a few things

*Notes on Ireland and Other Writings*

together, took the little brown donkey, and was ready for her perilous journey to Damascus. After briefly embracing Claudia, her father watched her disappear over the hill with tears in his eyes.

"Poor child," he said somberly. "No use to tell her that her grandfather is right in the Roman emperor's hand, and will never miss such a chance to curry favor as this. He will listen to her story, take the picture, put her in hiding for safety, and then tell the whole business to the emperor as an example of his loyalty. And that will be the end of her Messiah."

Shortly after she disappeared from sight, the old man sees two soldiers approaching. They tell him they want Claudia. Her father tells them that she has not yet returned from her trip to Bethlehem, and that he fears something has happened to her.

The soldiers don't believe him. "Oh really, old man?" One sneered. "So why have so many people in town reported to us that they saw her come home?"

The other soldier raised a fist as if to try to punch Jonathan in the face, but was halted by the first soldier.

"Never mind. He's in bad enough shape already. Come on. Time to start asking questions in town. Someone's bound to have seen where she is heading. And we have got to get her. It's her neck or ours."

Claudia and the donkey had headed slightly northeast, but now turned eastward. They had smooth sailing from Nazareth until now, and as they crossed the Hasbani river they could see Mt. Hermon looming above. But the weather was beginning to turn for the worse, as was Claudia's predicament.

She was planning to go around Mt. Hermon to reach Damascus. But as she stopped to rest for a moment, she looked to the left and saw Roman soldiers ahead. It was turning colder, the snow was heavier, and the wind was beginning to howl. She looked to the right and it seemed the coast was clear. Continuing on, she turned towards the south away from the soldiers to get around Mt. Hermon on that side. Even so, she knew from the appearance of those soldiers that her pursuers were closing in on her. Now if she could only get around the mountain, hopefully the coast would be clear on the final leg to Damascus.

Plodding slowly and numbly through the snowdrifts now, Claudia looked up and saw more soldiers. She both gasped and sighed in disbelief at the same time. They looked far away but she knew they were fairly close to her. She now could not go around the mountain on the south side. And she was sure the soldiers from the north had advanced further towards her.

Nonetheless, she turned back towards the north, because getting around the mountain on that side would be easier than from the south. Her steps were even slower now, methodically lifting her right foot and placing it carefully, unfeelingly, before her left foot.

Claudia and the donkey had just about gotten to the north side of the mountain when she heard a shout. "There she is!"

The soldiers had spotted her. She wasn't sure if they had spotted her before, but they definitely had now. Struggling to see and even move, she looked and saw that the soldiers were getting closer. She finally decided that the only way through was to try to somehow climb the mountain and skirt along its side towards the east, or at least find some concealment and shelter from the oncoming soldiers, and from the terrible storm. Those were the two main priorities right now.

For several hours, Claudia and the donkey searched the base of the mountain for a navigable way upward. Finally she found a narrow track which looked like it had been used recently. Little did she know that it had been — by Joseph, Mary and Jesus.

Very thankful for her discovery, she and the donkey began the way up the mountain. She lost all virtual track of time in her desperation to find a place to rest and hide from her pursuers. For now, getting to Damascus will have to wait. But she was still determined to get there.

Down below at the base of the mountain, the soldiers had converged and were meeting. One looked up towards the mountaintop, and then strained his eyes towards the other soldiers, and then spoke.

"She is on her way up the mountain. She has no chance. Come, let us go find shelter before we are caught in it." The other soldiers agreed and started back.

Claudia was so cold and tired that it seemed she could not bear it. The wind was getting colder now, and she was in an agony of numbness. But, floundering aimlessly along the narrow trail, she surprisingly began to feel warmer and more drowsy. Slowly but surely she and the donkey were making solid progress up the mountain.

Finding a narrow crack in the rock, she stopped to rest. Though she was warmer, she was also more drowsy. "Before I go to sleep, and just in case I don't get to Damascus, I will write my grandfather a letter," she said. "Many climbers come around here. I am sure someone would find it."

She got out some papyrus and struggled with the storm, but managed to finish the letter and put it in her coat pocket. She then gazed out and then down the mountain.

Instinct told her of the folly of turning back. When the weather improved, the soldiers would be waiting for her. They would never give up pursuing her. Claudia and the donkey headed back on the path slowly up the mountain.

"The king's sycophants," she thought grimly, "will never accept going back to him empty-handed."

Claudia and the donkey came to a turn along the narrow path, and immediately after the turn the path went sharply upward. Thankfully it did not go sharply upward for long, and finally they stopped climbing and the path somewhat flattened out in the side of the mountain.

Wearily she raised her hand, wiped the snow from her face and brushed some hair from her eyes, and stood motionless. And then she saw it.

About fifty feet away, under a narrow and low overhang, was a tiny opening to a cave. Claudia could not believe her good fortune. She and the donkey stumbled to the opening and it was just large enough to shelter them until the worst of the storm could pass.

Sighing with comfort, she and the donkey huddled together for warmth. Suddenly she noticed something on the side of the little cave wall. She reached over to it, and it was a small bundle. She gasped in disbelief when opened the bundle. It was a piece of stone tablet with the words "The Messiah was here" written on it.

She wondered in amazement. Had Jesus been in this cave? She did not know it but he had, with Joseph and Mary, and Mary had written the message on the tablet. It was also their narrow path that Claudia had taken up to the cave.

Claudia placed the tablet back in the bundle and set it back along the cave wall. She also took the portrait and the letter to her grandfather out of her coat pockets and placed them inside the bundle and wrapped the bundle up again. A much better place for them, she thought.

She now felt comfortable warmth and desperately needed rest. Her donkey was already asleep.

Just as she was about to drift off to sleep, she said to herself, "Tomorrow I shall find my way again, and will be in Damascus in no time at all."

She fell asleep, and slept soundly. And so it was that she never heard the roar of the avalanche of snow and ice that roared down the mountainside. Claudia, the donkey, and the bundle were buried by the slide, to wait almost 2000 years to be found.

\* \* \* \*

It is the year 1948, about four months after Israel becomes a nation. A great discovery has been made on the northwest side of Mt. Hermon.

The Bedouin told Martin, an archaeologist, that another archaeologist had hired him as a guide up the mountain. For years other archaeologists had hired him and other locals for help with the climb, especially at this time of year. The season was hot and there were many slides.

One of these slides had caught the archaeologist and carried him into a crevasse, breaking his leg. The guide had managed to avoid the slide. As the slide passed it had gathered snow and ice of many years and carried it away. When the slide had passed the narrow overhang, the little cave was revealed and also the great discovery was revealed.

"What is this other man's name?" Martin asked. "We must go see him."

"His name is Ferguson," said the Bedouin. "Let us go see him. He wants a return trip up the mountain again as soon as possible."

Arriving at Ferguson's and entering his office, they could tell his leg was still not healed and he was still limping, and that he would not be able to climb up the mountain himself.

"What is this fantastic discovery?" Martin asked eagerly.

"That will not be revealed until you reach it. Even though my guide is going with you I want the utmost of silence," replied Ferguson. "I want silence until the excavation is completed."

He looked down for a moment and then looked at Martin. "I asked you to come from your work at Baalbek because you

*Notes on Ireland and Other Writings*

may be able to decipher some writing for me. It looks to me about 2000 years old."

Martin and the Bedouin guide began their journey. As they trudged up the snowy slope, Martin began to question his sanity. He could tell that Ferguson was very excited about his discovery. To climb the mountain, with the danger of more slides, and not be told what was there?

But the Bedouin guide and Ferguson seemed honest, and of course it took very little to put his archaeological nose to the scent. The lure of such a great discovery was not to be passed up.

They had been climbing for several hours, and Martin needed to rest. It wasn't much farther, as they were just about to come to the turn in the path.

Martin was beginning to feel very excited, and he looked ahead with much anticipation.

After climbing upward, they came to the narrow and low overhang and then the entrance to the small cave.

"We are here," said the guide. He surveyed the scene. "Nothing has been moved or touched."

Martin moved forward a few steps. The interior of the cave was mostly filled with ice. The guide moved forward and beck-

*Notes on Ireland and Other Writings*

oned Martin. For a minute Martin saw nothing. Then he gasped in amazement. He saw her.

Held fast in the shelter of her icy cavern, was a teenage girl. She was lying, seemingly asleep, with her head pillowed on the rump of a small donkey who also was seemingly asleep.

The girl was perfectly preserved in the ice. Even her clothing from the Biblical days seemed to be so.

Martin wanted to speak but was having difficulty finding words. Finally he managed.

"My God, what a find! This is simply amazing. I think Ferguson was about right with the date. From her clothing I would guess she has been her 2000 years."

The guide smiled at him. "I bet this is worth the trip up the mountain."

"No doubt about that," said Martin. "And also worth the silence." He studied the girl and the ice some more. The girl had a high forehead, perfectly formed features, and overall an expression of nobility. He was still astounded that both she and the donkey seemed so well preserved.

"We will have to contact the other men at Baalbek at once," Martin said. "We can't risk getting that ice away from her without proper equipment, and they have the right equipment for he job. My God, man. What a discovery. Perhaps we will be famous, and perhaps be able to make many more expeditions." His voice still quivered in the excitement.

"It was Ferguson who first found her," reminded the guide. "Perhaps you can share if you complete the excavation."

"Yes, I know." Martin wiped his brow and looked at the guide. "Ferguson mentioned writing, that I may need to decipher something."

"Ah yes," the Bedouin guide said. "The amazing discovery is not merely the girl and her donkey." He reached over to the cave wall and gave the archaeologist the bundle wrapped in animal hide. "When Ferguson and I came it was in a few inches of ice. But we were able to take a pick and chip away at the ice and slowly dislodge it. It seems almost perfectly preserved as well."

Martin opened the bundle and removed the contents one by one. First was the small stone tablet. He read the inscription and wondered in amazement. "Jesus was here!" he exclaimed aloud. Then he stared ahead for a moment, thinking of being in the same cave as the Messiah. He really

*Notes on Ireland and Other Writings*

couldn't believe it. And this was on top of finding the girl and donkey so preserved in the ice.

After removing the tablet, Martin took out a piece of silk about twenty inches square. As he unrolled it, another item fell to the ground. He picked it up and it was a roll of papyrus covered with small writing.

Martin's excitement was beginning to simmer, though he still could not believe these amazing discoveries. But he was becoming again a man of science.

The papyrus manuscript had an ancient texture which seemed to take him back to when it was written. Looking closely, he began trying to decipher the writing. A lot of the writing was not clear but he read what he could:

"To my most honored grandfather," Martin began from the papyrus. "I cannot assure that I will see you in Damascus....I am pursued ruthlessly....to destroy what I bear with me....I shall try to elude capture....I will be able to secrete myself....the treasure I carry....which the world must have. Dearest Grandfather, when I painted the child in the stable, I was giving the world a portrait of the Messiah....it bears heavily upon me that I must guard with my life the safety of that portrait."

Martin had trouble reading that part of the message and could not make out the whole message, but was able to decipher enough to understand it. But what was this portrait? Where was it?

He continued reading from the papyrus as best he could. "And so, I beg of you, Grandfather, that if by some mischance I never reach you, and the portrait is brought to you in Damascus, I humbly ask you to please bear it with you when you return to Rome. Please intercede with your great friend the emperor, and protect the child who has come to save. He is a threat to their sovereignty."

There was more writing on the papyrus, but Martin decided to try to decipher the rest later. He retrieved the piece of silk and noticed there was something on the other side of the silk. He spread it out examine it closer. The Bedouin guide came over as well. It was then they saw that a picture had been painted upon it.

The picture depicted some sort of room, very poorly furnished. There was a beautiful and young woman holding a baby in front to a manger. A slightly older man stood beside her, and he was gazing at the child. There were three richly dressed men also in the room, as well as several poorly dressed men carrying shepherd's crooks. Over at the side of the picture were some stalls with cows in them, and some other animals were in the room as well. Over the whole scene there seemed to be painted some sort of haze, or glow of light, which brightened the background of the portrait.

Martin and the guide looked at the painting for quite some time without uttering a sound. Then they gazed at each other, but still said nothing.

Martin finally looked around the cave and surveyed everything, trying to take it all in. "I really can't believe all of this," he said.

"That is exactly how I felt the first time I came up here," the guide agreed.

"We had better get back to see Ferguson and also get more men up here to try to get the girl out of the ice," Martin said.

It was getting late and so the two men slept in the cave that night, but were on their way early the next morning. Martin took the bundle with him that carried the stone tablet, Claudia's letter to her grandfather and her portrait of the room in the stable from the night Jesus was born.

He and the Bedouin guide made it back to Ferguson, and they talked amongst each other, still amazed at the find. They made

*Notes on Ireland and Other Writings*

plans to continue the excavation and to try to get the girl out of the ice.

But before more men could go up the mountain to continue the excavation, another avalanche of snow and ice roared down the mountainside and buried the girl and her donkey once more.

\*    \*    \*    \*

# EDITOR'S FINAL NOTE

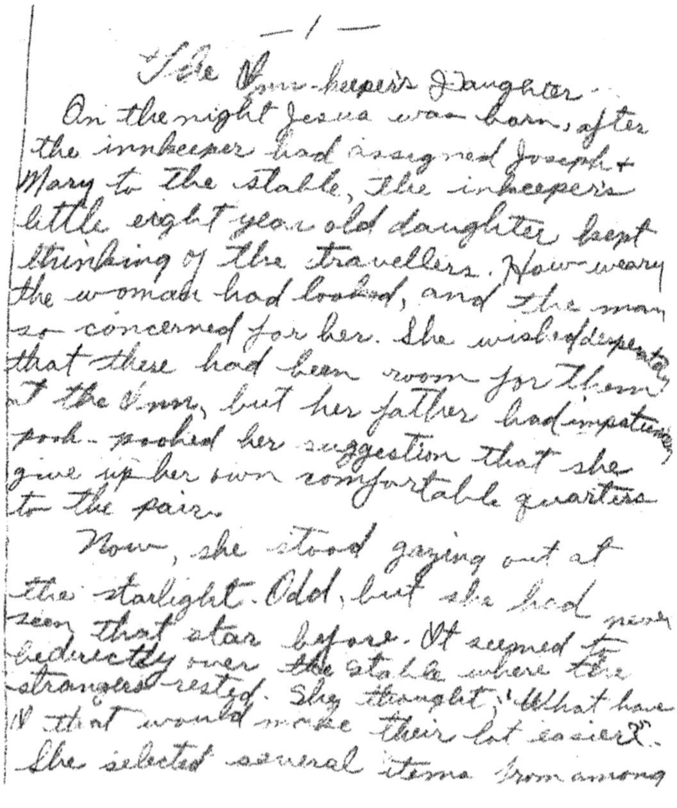

— 1 —

The Inn-keeper's Daughter

On the night Jesus was born, after the innkeeper had assigned Joseph & Mary to the stable, the innkeeper's little eight year old daughter kept thinking of the travellers. How weary the woman had looked, and the man so concerned for her. She wished desperately that there had been room for them at the Inn, but her father had impatiently pooh-poohed her suggestion that she give up her own comfortable quarters to the pair.

Now, she stood gazing out at the starlight. Odd, but she had never seen that star before. It seemed to be directly over the stable where the strangers rested. She thought, "What have I that would make their lot easier?" She selected several items from among

This is a sample of my aunt's handwriting.

*Notes on Ireland and Other Writings*

On October 21, 2010, I went down to Centralia and then down to Frances. I stopped in Centralia and put some flowers on my aunt Nancy's grave and the other family graves. I also said a quick hello to my aunt and told her that I was making a book of her writings. Hopefully she would be pleased, and pleased with the editing I have done with her writings.

After visiting Centralia, the next stop was Frances....turning off I-5 onto Hwy. 6. As luck would have it, there was work being done on the road and I and other cars were basically stopped for 15 minutes. Reaching the town of Doty, I wanted to stop at Rainbow Falls State Park. I had seen it on the map and read some on the internet and it sounded interesting. There was also a large sign right off I-5 mentioning the state park, as if it were a very popular tourist attraction, or as if it was being promoted as such.

However, the road into the state park was closed because a new bridge was being built. So I had to go into town and drive all the way around, and on two or three different roads trying to find the place. After about an hour there was finally a sign and I turned in. There had not been a sign coming the other way. I parked in one of the spots and walked to the falls. As it turned out, the falls were right next to Hwy. 6 and the falls were not really falls. What was there was basically just a small rapid. I spent an hour driving around to see what I expected would be a worthwhile sight, especially with a name like Rainbow Falls. But quite a disappointment.

After the little town of Doty came the town of Pe Ell. This is an actual town, with stores and restaurants. A very nice and quaint little town. Leaving the town the highway turned and I didn't turn, and I ended up on a little country bumpkin road heading into the hills. After awhile I finally found my way back to Hwy. 6 and continued west toward Frances.

About 12 miles west of Pe Ell came Frances. I slowed down to try to take it in, since this is where my aunt and grandmother had lived for a few years. Frances now was just a bunch of buildings, and some up on the hill, with a church right off the highway. It was set in the Willapa Hills as my aunt described. I found Fern Creek and took the little road among the properties, and then turned back on to the highway.

Heading back out of Frances, I stopped at the church. My aunt said that the

*Notes on Ireland and Other Writings*

church was set halfway up a hill, and that there was a steep grade leading to a cemetery above the church. Sure enough, that was the case. I parked and walked up the steep grade to the cemetery above the church. I walked through to see if I could find any ancestors or friends that my aunt had mentioned in her writings. Before I left, I took in the view. The narrow valley below, and the Willapa Hills above. Very quiet, very beautiful, very peaceful.

All in all, it was pretty much still as my aunt described.

Once again, I hope you have enjoyed reading my aunt's writings.

A portion of the proceeds of this book will go to fight glaucoma and charities to help the blind.

Jim Berwick, Nancy Hennessy's nephew

CPSIA information can be obtained at www.ICGtesting.com
231603LV00005B/39/P